Users Researching Health and Social Care: An Empowering Innovation?

Shulamit Ramon

VENTURE PRESS

BASW website: http://www.basw.co.uk

Published by
VENTURE PRESS
16 Kent Street
Birmingham
B5 6RD

British Library Cataloguing-in-Publication Data
A catalogue record for this book is available from the British Library

ISBN   1 86178 057 5   (paperback)

Cover design by:
Western Arts
21b Highgate Close
London
N6 4SD

Printed in Great Britain

To David, wherever you are, for your generosity of spirit

Contents

Page

List of Tables   Page

Acknowledgement

This book is dedicated to David Brandon, the editor of the series, *Theories in Social Work*, who died in November 2001 after a short illness. David was a supportive editor, who did not hesitate to offer constructive criticism while improving the author's style. He was himself a gifted and prolific writer on social work, advocacy, homelessness, mental illness and health, spirituality and Buddhism.

I had the privilege of working with him on developing a strategy for mental health promotion for Havering and Barking at the time he became ill. David's contribution veered from being inspirational in setting the scene for a dialogue day with community groups to telling rude jokes; from searching the Internet to polite, yet unflinching, criticism of some of the services he visited as part of getting to know the area.

David was a user of mental health services as a young man; a fact he has never forgotten to disclose or to learn from throughout his creative and turbulent life. I hope he would have been proud to see a book on user research published in a series he edited. I shall miss him as an editor.

I wish to thank the users who have participated in the projects I have taken part in, those who worked in the projects the other authors of this book describe, and those who are among the authors of this book. I am all too pleased that this list is long... The fact that half of the authors are also users of health and social care services speaks volume about what has been achieved since the mid-1990s in terms of advancing user research.

In particular, I wish to thank the authors of this book for their readiness to share with the readers and me their labour of love.

Vicky Thompson helped greatly in shaping the manuscript; Christine Sedgwick and Lyn Nock at Venture Press helped in ensuring the early publication of the book at a crisis period for the series.

List of Contributors

Lesley Allen
Service user and co-editor of *Personality Disorder North Essex News*.

Lisa Baxter
Service user, Folk.us research network, Department of Psychology, University of Exeter.

Avril Butler
Lecturer in Social Work, School of Social Work, University of Plymouth and service user.

Heather Castillo
Manager, Colchester Mind advocacy project, researcher and co-editor of *Personality Disorder North Essex News*.

Judy Dean
Manager, mental health rehabilitation services, Addenbrooke's NHS Trust, Cambridge.

Barbara Fawcett
Lecturer in Social Work, School of Applied Social Studies, University of Bradford. Researcher into disability and feminist issues.

Jeanette Harding
Service user, Lifecraft telephone helpline supervisor, independent trainer and social worker, Cambridge.

Anna Reima Maglijlic
Research fellow, Healthnet International, Sarajevo. Social worker and researcher; co-ordinator of user forum, Sarajevo, Bosnia.

Annie Mitchell
Lecturer in Community Psychology, Department of Psychology, University of Exeter.

Hannah Morrow
Disability Rights Project director, Newmarket; service user; and previously co-ordinator of CamAdvocat, Cambridge.

Joanna Payne
Service user, and carer development project co-ordinator, Barnet Social Services, Barnet.

Avigdor Petrank
Israeli user research project co-ordinator, service user, Ph.D. in Physics.

Rachel Purtell
Co-ordinator, Folk.us research network, Department of Psychology, University of Exeter and service user.

Shulamit Ramon
Professor of Interprofessional Health and Social Studies, School of Community Health and Social Studies, Anglia Polytechnic University, Cambridge; researcher, social worker and clinical psychologist.

Tim Schafer
Senior Lecturer in Mental Health Nursing, School of Community Health and Social Studies, Anglia Polytechnic University, Chelmsford.

Vered Slonim-Nevo
Professor of Social Work, Ben Gurion University, Beer Sheva, Israel, social worker, family therapist and researcher.

Israel J. Sykes
Chair, Benafeshainu (In Our Soul) a user and carer organisation based in Jerusalem, social worker, researcher at the Brookedale Institute, Jerusalem.

Introduction

Who should read this book?

Why should practitioners be interested in user research?

Frontline practitioners of health and social care, and their managers, are busy people. They feel that too much is demanded of them, with too few financial, structural and human resources available to meet the demands made on them by the organisation in which they work, the clients, or the government.

Practitioners are often demoralised by this state of affairs, compounded as it is by:

- Frequent reorganisation of the service in which they work, imposed either from above or outside the organisation, and invariably without their involvement;
- The suffering of the users with whom they are working and the difficulty of resolving satisfactorily the number of the problems they face;
- The imbalance between care and control in everyday practice, where the increased emphasis on risk as a negative aspect of human lives leads to the elimination of positive risk-taking;
- The ever-increasing bureaucratic accountability leading to an escalation in paperwork and red tape, further consuming the time of practitioners, and limiting not only the time and energy available to be spent on users, but also their discretionary power and professional autonomy; and
- The effect of globalisation and technocratisation of professional work. (Dominelli and Hoogvelt, 1996)

While the government, and the research establishment, emphasise the need for evidence as to the efficacy of the methods practitioners apply in their work, the latter see this focus as an unjustified attack on their competence and a further attempt to curtail their fragile level of autonomy within a bureaucratised system. Recommendations for changes in practice patterns culled from research findings are rarely followed by practitioners, and are often dismissed as coming from those too far removed from everyday practice to understand what the problems are (Everitt *et al.*, 1992).

Yet it is not often that practitioners acknowledge the high level of uncertainty of their own knowledge, and the role this may play in adding to the thorny issues outlined above. Using any type of evidence such uncertainty is rife within social care – where too many factors are working simultaneously for any coherent, consistent and predictable outcome to be satisfactorily achieved in the over-busy, over-stressed, life of a practitioner. This applies equally to health care, where all too often context issues are overlooked in favour of health technology considerations.

1

Uncertainty can play a positive part in motivating practitioners to tune their responses to the specific context, and to shy away from simplistic and rigid responses. Paying attention to the multiplicity of factors impinging on the welfare arena is another bonus, as is the readiness to reassess the value of an earlier response to a similar, but not identical, situation (Fook, 2000).

Yet the call for evidence-based practice is justified in principle because of the price paid by users, practitioners and society when uncertain knowledge applied to decision-making leads to mistakes which wreck people's lives. Improvements aimed at reducing this cost, and reducing trial and error, should be welcomed by all those involved. However, codifying evidence as good enough by a national institute such as the National Institute for Clinical Excellence (NICE) runs the risk of stifling the development of contextualised response to uncertainty mentioned above, as well as that of innovative practice.

Most practitioners use a mixture of some evidence-based and some practice-wisdom-based knowledge in reaching their decisions. Some of them argue that practice wisdom is a safer base because it is a distillation of their own knowledge and that of colleagues they trust. In doing so, they tell us that it is the *credibility* of the source of knowledge that is the key to whether a practitioner will use it or not.

Of course, the more critical the evidence, the more defensive practitioners become – and the less likely to implement it. Thus the need to engage practitioners in research meaningful to them which provides knowledge that they accept as credible, is the key to the likely implementation of research findings (Reason, 1994). Indeed, for far too long both frontline workers and users have been largely ignored by researchers as stakeholders whose views should count as relevant, essential knowledge.

For far too long both groups have been ignored as partners to research, to the creation of not only new facets of knowledge but also of the questions to be asked and the methodologies with which to pursue the search for answers. Yet practitioners too have been slow to see a positive role for research in contributing to their knowledge, and to push forward opportunities for participatory research.

This book centres on users' involvement in research, but it does not ignore the importance of frontline workers' engagement in research as active participants, exemplified in Chapters 3, 4, 5 and 9. These highlight instances of workers' involvement in research in innovative and imaginative ways.

In addition, practitioners should be interested in users' perspectives, provided in each of the chapters of this book, as well as in user-researchers, because of the healthy interdependency that exists between practitioners and users. For their work, practitioners depend on users' knowledge for the purposes of:

- Making sense of what happens to users;
- How best to listen to them;
- The how and what of good support;
- How to deal with their part in solving users' problems;
- Assessing motivation for change and utilising it;
- Establishing good working relationships;
- Getting feedback which enables practitioners to work more effectively;
- Extending their knowledge;
- Getting information that helps to improve service structures;
- Getting information relevant to policy and legislative changes; and
- Establish and create more meaningful research agendas and research projects.

While a number of the above-listed purposes relate to both individual and collective levels of user – practitioner interaction, some of the objectives are best met at the latter level, in which both practitioners and users come together as collectives. These include meaningful research agendas and projects, as well as working for service structures, policy and legislative changes.

Practitioners can thus gain from user research, even though it may include a critique of their own work. Good user research does not simply stop at criticising practitioners' performance, but provides insight beyond this, into underlying factors, such as the effect of labelling, stigmatisation, lack of resources, fragmentation, discontinuity and abuse. It will also pinpoint the qualities of good, supportive services and their providers (for examples, see Chapters 6, 7, 8, 9 and 10).

Why should researchers be interested in user research?
On the surface, user research, and user researchers, pose a challenge and offer competition to professional researchers and the research they conduct. This type of research certainly challenges the view that professional researchers are necessarily the only group that should carry out research into health and social care, as it based on the assumptions that:

- Service users' understanding of their own experiences of issues and services is a valid perspective. It is important for good research to obtain it as an aspect of knowledge that equals that of other stakeholders in this field;
- Users should play a central part in deciding what the research questions and methods should be, as well as in analysing data and presenting it, given that the stated primary aim of research in this field is to improve their lives; and

3

- User researchers carry more credibility in the eyes of other users – as participants rather than as professional researchers.

These issues are further explored in the first chapter of this book.

The above discussion indicates that, in addition to the challenge, user research offers an innovative approach to research, likely to appeal to researchers who doubt the validity of traditional positivistic research, and accept the usefulness of an interpretative perspective. It would also appeal to researchers who have been concerned with the imbalance of power between those traditionally researched (often referred to in the literature as 'the subjects') and the researchers, in terms of lack of input by the first group into any phase of the research process. In traditional research, even when the research includes a component asking them about their experiences of health and social care problems and services, this is structured and carried out within the parameters defined by the researchers.

Competition is an issue where users wish to be the *only* researchers; that is, when separatism rules over partnership, when users are afraid that they will be taken over by professional researchers, and when the structure of the project does not ensure that this cannot happen (Evans and Fisher, 1998). Given the newness of user research projects, co-optation may be a more realistic fear for users rather than them competing with professional researchers.

User research poses another challenge for those researchers who believe in its intrinsic merits – how to prepare users to carry out high-quality research in a fairly short time, especially in comparison with the length of time it has taken professional researchers to train. Chapter 1 examines this issue, and examples of how this challenge has been met are to be found in almost every chapter of this book.

Why should service users and carers be interested in user research?
Users and carers have often spoken and written about the neglect of their perspectives by professionals. Moreover, some have commented how their views have been perceived as invalid by the latter. Users and carers see this neglect as detrimental to good practice and to achieving the aim of providing them with good support (Barnes and Bowl, 2001; Jones, 2001).

Yet rarely have users and carers commented on the fact that most research in health and social care has either ignored users' and carers' perspectives or approached these only from within the researchers' viewpoint. This is in part because of the lack of recognition of the role research plays in determining policy and practice by users and carers; in part due to the remoteness of research from everyday services; and most of them might never have participated in a research project, met a researcher, or read a research report.

For users and carers to be asked to become active partners in research is tantamount to a paradigm shift in terms of their rightful place in the health and social care system – from being the underdog to becoming a respected associate. It is also a vindication of the validity of their perspective, as well as a testimony of their potential ability to become researchers. Yet, given the real and perceived remoteness of research, interest in it is likely to be reserved for the more articulate user and carer. The deep mistrust many users and carers have developed about the service systems over the years will also contribute to research remaining a minority interest, rather than a recognition by the majority of this radical shift in direction.

What is in the book: the horizons of user research.
This book does not attempt to cover all existing user research projects in the United Kingdom. Its authors celebrate the development of user research that took place in the 1990s, and the innovative work that has place around it, to which the authors of this book have also contributed.

The threat that only lip service will be paid towards this type of research, and the continuous attempts to brand it as either 'unscientific' or 'unrepresentative', should be remembered and challenged, if user research is to thrive in the 2000s. This book offers a patchwork of text in which each chapter describes a different facet of inclusive user research, mostly participative, and user-led. Contributions were selected on the basis of their innovative value to this undertaking. The accounts attempt to offer realistic and analytical perspectives, written with a minimal use of jargon, and an easily accessible style. They describe processes and outcomes, ways of organising user research, issues researched, methodologies and methods. While pleased with what has been achieved, they also look at the expected and unexpected obstacles and opportunities to the development of high-quality user research, outlining the lessons learned and the value added to the various stakeholders, as well as health and social care service systems, upon which this endeavour has had an impact.

The stakeholders include:
- User researchers;
- User participants;
- Carers;
- Practitioners;
- Managers;
- Professional researchers;
- Educators;

- Policy makers;
- Research funding organisations; and
- Local and national politicians.

The book begins with a overview chapter by Shulamit Ramon (researcher, social work and mental health educator) in which the assumptions, beliefs, hopes and fears of user research are explored, moving on to investigate the reality of practising it. The text highlights the ongoing dilemmas of users doing research in partnership with professional researchers.

Joanna Payne (user, development officer, social worker by training) offers a moving account of how she has allowed herself to reflect. She came to reflection after twelve years in which this felt to be impossible, because of the impact of mental illness. She explains how the exercise of reflection helped her to research herself within a safe environment. Her contribution demonstrates that, far from being intimidated by the other members of the group who did not define themselves as users, but who were ready to share their doubts and vulnerabilities, she has experienced the group, and not only the reflective process itself, as a source of positive support.

Avril Butler (social work educator and user) – coming from narrative and biographical methods – writes about the use of creative autobiography as a research tool for a group of women, staff and users, to explore, reintegrate and share different aspects of their lives. Using a multimedia approach, her own vulnerability as a springboard for the group, and the safe haven offered by the group, enabled each group member to explore the private and the public, the personal and the professional, to both comment and control involvement. This chapter raises central issues about the co-involvement of salaried staff alongside users, when both use identical methods and themselves in the process of being research participants.

Vered Slonim-Nevo (social work educator, researcher and family therapist) illuminates the systematic evaluation of planned cognitive behavioural intervention as a shared undertaking between the therapist/social worker and the client, where the latter becomes a co-researcher as much as the former. The evaluation component enables not only the systematic assessment of what went on in the intervention from the perspective of the client; it also incorporates a redistribution of power relationships in the unequal balance of power that most clinical interventions express, in which clients are empowered to express their views on the clinician's performance as much as on what the intervention has or has not achieved. Engaging in the exercise of selecting the evaluation methods adds a dimension of intellectual partnership to the shared project.

Barbara Fawcett's (researcher and social work educator) contribution highlights how a community project, focused on solutions to unemployment in a multiracial city, 'slips' into an action research mode in which project members are active participants. Aimed at engaging users from Asian groups and practitioners from health and social care, this European Union (EU)-sponsored project demonstrates the viability of participative and inclusive evaluation – even though it was not carried out by user researchers – as an integral component of the project, clearly enhancing it in more than one way. The evaluation is used to market the project, to report to its funders, to map outcomes and their value for the participants, and to generate change in the project. The focus on an approach sensitive to ethnicity and gender in the services on offer to the participants, and in its evaluation, is a central feature of this project. This reminds us of the need to take context-specific factors into consideration in any inclusive health and social care initiative, and the clear benefits of doing so.

Judy Dean (health manager with a nursing background), Jeanette Harding (user activist and former social worker) and Hannah Morrow (advocate and user) describe a complex project in which users living in the community undertook the interviewing of users living in long-stay wards in the local hospital to add a more holistic and emphatic element to the traditional assessment for the resettlement in the community of the latter. The interview schedule focused on the positive and negative aspects of hospital living, and hopes and fears relating to life outside it. The interviewers, most of whom had themselves previously experienced being admitted to the same hospital, were keen to learn the skills of interviewing and become involved. A short, yet intensive and supportive, training programme sufficed. Their sense of achievement, being paid well for the job, the acknowledgement by the link staff that the user-researchers have reached the long-stay residents much better than anticipated, more than compensated for the uncomfortable moments of reliving their own experiences and meeting people in hospital who had remained there since their own past admissions.

Heather Castillo (advocacy project manager and researcher) and Lesley Allan (user and editor of a newsletter on personality disorder) map the first project in which people with personality disorder interview others with the same-label disorder to make sense of the experiences of being given the diagnosis, of relevant life events, identified strength and difficulties, usefulness or otherwise of different types of support, and their wishes for support. The user-researchers of this project have disseminated it and the findings widely, and have established a regional newsletter since the completion of the project. As this label is rapidly overtaking schizophrenia in terms of public and government demonisation, it is of particular importance that the intellectual abilities and humanity of people labelled thus is also recognised.

Reima (Rea) Maglijlic's (researcher and social work educator) project focuses on researching social work education from the perspectives of three stakeholders: clients of social workers; students; and social work practitioners. In this context the students are users too, while the practitioners are the 'finished product' of that educational process, who communicate what they know to their clients and to students in practice placements. Using co-operative inquiry principles and methods, the project also offers a cross-cultural perspective, by comparing the views and processes of interaction of the stakeholders in Cambridge (UK) and Sarajevo (Bosnia), which, interestingly, led to some different, and unexpected, outcomes. The fact that the three stakeholders could collaborate well within the framework of this project illustrates the potential for such collaboration within research and education, provided it is well supported.

Tim Schafer's (nurse educator and researcher) study of empowerment in different settings set out to explore whether there are indeed setting components that make users feel more empowered, or less. Using questionnaires validated in the USA, he aimed to revalidate them through the active involvement of a local user forum and the feedback of the research participants. His statistical analysis has enabled a map of variables to emerge which contribute to the sense of empowerment. Thus this work helps us to clarify the rather elusive concept of empowerment.

Avigdor Petrank (user activist with a Ph.D. in Physics) and Israel Sykes (user leader and social work professional researcher) introduce us to the first user research project in Israel, focused on the experiences of admission and re-entry to the community. Their account demonstrates what it takes to establish the first such project in a country, in terms of encouraging the necessary cultural shift among professionals, users and carers. Some interesting alliances were formed, such as between the user group involved, an Israeli researcher working in the UK, local researchers/educators in social work, psychiatrists, and some social workers. Some other social workers became very defensive at the prospect of user-led research.

At this initial stage, the project raises more questions than answers, including: What are the opportunities and the obstacles that came to the surface, as a result of this initiative? Can such an innovation be promoted by a partnership of 'insiders' and 'outsider', as was the case here? What are the necessary and sufficient conditions for the success of such a project? How can its sustainability and continuation be assured? and What are the lessons to be learned from this experiment?

The chapter by Rachel Purtell (user activist), Lisa Baxter (user activist) and Annie Mitchell (Lecturer in Community Psychology) completes the contributions to the book. They have established Folk.us, a user–researcher network in Exeter (UK). The text outlines the aims, process and first outcomes of this endeavour. Theirs is a story about stimulating interest in research while demystifying it, attempting to create a culture of research that would promote the status of evidence-based practice. The new culture of research would give users, carers, and other lay and professional people, an equal say in what type of research is conducted and how it would be conducted, and its findings applied in practice, aiming at relevant and high-quality research. A tool of *community capacity* building, the project – supported by both local health and social care agencies – has constructed a number of stimulating steps to further these objectives. The account gives us a taste of the obstacles and opportunities for truly collaborative research partnership.

The richness of the different contributions to the book, all of them innovative, and the clear applications to the practice of many of the process and outcome findings, will, it is hoped, attract practitioners, researchers, users and carers to be among the readers of this book, as well as also educators, policy-makers and research funders.

User research is not a bed of roses, as this book will attest, but it is hoped that those who are sceptical about its potential will permit themselves to read the accounts offered in the text with an open mind as to its promise.

References

Barnes, M and Bowl, R (2001) *Taking Over the Asylum: Empowerment and Mental Health*, Basingstoke, Palgrave

Dominelli, L and Hoogvelt, A (1996) 'Globalisation and the nocratisation of social work', *Critical Social Policy*, 47, pp 45–62

Evans, C and Fisher, M (1998) 'Collaborative evaluation with service users' in: Shaw, I and Lishman, J (eds) *Evaluation and Social Work Practice*, London, Sage

Everitt, A, Hardiker, P, Littlewood, J and Mullender, A (1992) *Applied Research for Better Practice*, Basingstoke, Macmillan

Fook, J (2000) 'Deconstructing and reconstructing professional expertise' in: Fawcett, B, Featherstone, B, Fook, J and Rossiter, A (eds) *Practice + Research in Social Work: Postmodernism Feminist Perspectives*, London, Routledge, pp 104–19

Jones, D (2001) *Myths, Madness and the Family: The impact of mental illness on families*, Basingstoke, Palgrave

Reason, P (1994) *Participation in Human Inquiry*, London, Sage

CHAPTER 1
User Research: Reflection and Action
Shulamit Ramon

We have been here for two hours. H, C, P, L and H have summarised the research and its findings, illustrating the largely negative impact of the label on those to whom it was attributed. More than 80 per cent reported being abused. They have also read extracts from each other's diaries, detailing the complex tale of abuses, losses, depression, despair and hope.

When they had finished, the chair invited questions and comments. There are none. C, who now works for the Trust in an administrative capacity, but has been a service user, tries to stimulate a discussion. Nothing happens. N. has another go, by raising an issue highlighted by the findings. No response.

I try too, a bit more aggressively, hoping to get a response. Then J, the well respected principle psychologist, says: 'All we can do now is to absorb what we have heard. Please do not push us any further.'

Another silence.

The user researchers present flowers to H and to psychiatrist who spoke about the relationships between the diagnostic category and post traumatic stress disorder; everyone claps. The seminar has come to its official end.

J. was right; it takes a lot out of professionals to take in the tale of abuses, losses, depression and despair, sprinkled with some hope, when they feel they have been active partners in it, and as responsible for the outcomes as the user/patient/client. Perhaps J and her colleagues have never before listened to the collective, yet authentic, voice of accumulated turmoil. Perhaps the impressive joint ability of the group to put across that experience, partly their own, partly that of the others they have interviewed, made it all the more poignant.

This chapter will look at the value, conceptual and methodological bases of user research, while paying attention to what is involved in actually carrying it out, without which user research risks remaining an unfulfilled wish, the domain of an isolated minority, shelved by the lip service paid to it by officialdom.

Examples are taken from projects in which I have been involved, and reflect the everyday reality of carrying out participative user research.

Recent history
The recent developments and interest in user research are related closely to the success of the disability movement in making compelling the case that users are people not only with abilities, but also with considerable experience,

whose lessons are largely hidden from professionals by users themselves, some researchers, some research funding organisations, and some politicians (Swain *et al.*, 1993; Barnes and Bowl, 2001).

The political focus on social inclusion which pertains at the time of writing also to disabled people, and inclusionary citizenship, coming from Europe and the USA to Britain, is already an outcome of this achievement, as well as of economic considerations, and the – misguided – continuation of the belief in modernity as a worthwhile social enterprise (Barry and Hallett, 1998).

While we may be weary of the rhetorical tone of politicians' offerings regarding social inclusion, or the number of times we are told to develop 'a modern NHS/social care' in clearly postmodern times, this success amounts to a paradigm shift for disabled people in the way they see themselves, the way they approach 'able-bodied' people, and the way they would like their social inclusion to be.

Research by leaders of the disability movement has played an important part in this shift, as did the critical analysis contained in research on disability carried by others. These leaders have recognised the value and power of research in shaping knowledge, attitudes and practices (Oliver, 1992; Barnes and Mercer, 1997; Beresford and Wallcraft, 1997). A number of them have also concluded that only users should be involved in research on users' issues, a point looked at further below. In doing so, they followed in the footsteps of feminist and black activists who discovered the value of research as part of their struggle for equality of rights and opportunities, as well as fighting against prejudice (Chahal, 1999; Fawcett *et al.*, 2000).

The other important factor enabling user research has come with the shift in research from a monolithic and monopolistic model to a more fragmented, and somewhat more open-ended, framework. Users of health and social care services have invariably been engaged in reflective thinking whenever they have attempted to make sense of what was happening to them, and of the interventions applied by service providers. A minority has engaged in research on becoming qualified researchers, willing and able to learn from their personal experiences as service users, and believing that there are clear connections between the personal and the professional. Yet others wished to separate their personal experience of being a user from that of being a researcher, either because the personal felt too uncomfortable to be exposed, or because its subjective element was perceived as being unscientific, where the latter was synonymous with 'objectivised' knowledge.

Such a belief is an integral part of the positivistic research paradigm upon whose tenets all natural and social scientists were socialised until recently.

Most scientists and educated lay people have internalised the belief that positivism offers the 'Gold standard' of scientific research, with detachment from the area and people studied being a necessary, unquestioned, element (Popper, 1941; Campbell, 1963; Macdonald and Sheldon, 1992).

The other tradition, which does not negate the value of subjective versions as an inherent part of research, has existed since before the advance of the positivistic approach ('premodern'), during its supremacy ('modernity'), and has made a comeback with the reintroduction of the *interpretative* paradigm of research as a tool within mainstream social science research ('postmodernity').

However, whereas during modernity this type of research was shunned as being 'non-scientific', this label has been questioned and discarded by those who accept the validity of the interpretative approach (Hughes, 1990;Strauss and Corbin, 1990; Winter and Munn-Giddings, 2001), arguing that research rigour can cope with subjective and intersubjective perspectives. Usually referred to as the 'qualitative' approach, the term interpretative is more correct, enabling us to dispose of the assumed, and false, dichotomy between qualitative and quantitative methods in the context of this approach.

We live in interesting times, in which a number of research paradigms are competing for acceptability. The history of such a competition is as brutal as that of commercial competition today, even if more polite in expression (Kuhn, 1970). It remains to be seen whether different approaches to thinking about and doing research will be allowed to co-exist (which would signify the victory of postmodernism), or whether only one paradigm will be permitted (signifying the re-emergence of modernity).

This state of affairs is reflected, for example, in the fact that we have not yet reached the stage in which interpretative research is viewed as being equal in scientific power to that of the positivistic paradigm within mainstream health and social care research, as the former is at best perceived to be an 'exploratory' tool which, on its own, does not enable the reaching of conclusive answers to the research questions. Ethics committees which rightly have to sanction permission to carry out research with service users, continue to be staffed by professionals who are both suspicious of the interpretative approach and ignorant of it. Thus far, no attempt has been made in any such committee to ensure better representation of the interpretative approach. We shall come back to this issue, and other problematic features of ethics committees, below.

Yet for many researchers, doubts as to the value of positivistic research have led them towards accepting the interpretative paradigm as *the main alternative* to it. These doubts include:

- The negation by the paradigm of the impact of the context in which the researchers live, and work on their research;
- The process of positivistic inquiry does not enable the views of people most affected by the phenomenon studied to be heard;
- This elimination begins from the formulation of the research question, and is inherent in the different phases of the research process;
- Even when a study attempts to include people's perceptions, these are allowed only through the specific viewpoint of the researcher as to the parameters of the perspectives they may hold, reflected in the way questions are phrased, the options allowed for answers, the belief in the value of numerical scales often attached to grading answers, and the type of statistical analysis used, even before reaching the stage of analysing the data and disseminating the conclusions;
- The experimental method, the formulation of a null hypothesis, randomisation, and the equation of significance with statistical probability favoured by the adherents of the positivistic approach are not necessarily enabling researchers to get nearer the truth, especially in those areas where the meaning attached is both true and relative (Taylor and Thornicroft, 1996); and.
- In many instances, it is negated that beliefs and values held by the major stakeholders in the research area need to be an inherent part of the research. In other words, what is negated is that beliefs, values and vested interests play a significant part in decision-making concerning the development of any type of science. The current debate on genetic research and reproduction illuminates a number of such conflicts:
  - Between privately patented genes and the public interest;
  - How an indigenous population with a purer genetic makeup than that found in the First World were robbed of the monetary value of their own blood samples – and how they were not even informed why the blood samples were being taken from them;
  - Whether to allow cloning of human beings; and
  - Whether to extend human reproduction beyond its natural time limit.

While ethical issues loom large in these conflicts, it is important to recognise that these are not the only issues at stake. There are also issues about what research is about, and that *the context in which the researchers work and live has an impact on it.*

User research has taken one — bold – further step in this direction by emphasising the value of the contribution of service users as active researchers, when they are not professionally qualified as researchers, but when they are trained to meet specific research tasks and participate in the research process as a whole.

While the book begins with a reflective experience, and throughout the place of reflexive thinking is significant, the core of the contributions presented here is about the systematic study of an issue focused upon, using more than one method in the search for better answers, and an analysis of these new attempts at answers.

Furthermore, the user-researchers participating in the different projects described below were at times research participants, but are more prominent in this text in the capacity of being researchers making use of their considerable experience of being identified as having a disability or a problem of living, and being consumers of services, many over a long period of time.

Underpinning values

The approach taken here comes from the belief that this experience, often associated with stigma, whose bearers are perceived to be unproductive members of society and weaklings, is useful and productive in terms of enabling other users – and the rest of us – to make sense of it through research.

The claim that user-researchers add value to what other researchers can offer, questions the taken-for-granted epistemological wisdom prevalent in most social science research, let alone natural science research, that the neutrality and objectivity of the researcher is a desirable and necessary quality within researcher–researched relationships, and is essential for producing good research. It also takes further, and differently, the Weberian attempt to understand – where a comparative framework is proposed as the best solution for the need to achieve an understanding of others from their own perspective.

Not negating the usefulness of comparative perspectives as a tool in understanding better others and oneself, user-researchers apply their empathic understanding as a research instrument with which to pinpoint the important research questions versus the less important ones, reaching decisions about the suitability of some methods over others, and in reaching out to the research participants.

This fundamental shift has become possible with the move towards interpretative approaches in social sciences research, which have accepted that:

- Objectivity in research is a myth;
- It is one neither desirable nor necessary for the purpose of understanding the other, or of social systems;
- Researchers need to be aware of their own beliefs ('biases') and acknowledge these;

- The research methodology has to enable the participants to speak as much as possible in their own voices;
- Research can be oppressive, as the power of the researcher is more prominent than that of the participants. Yet it can also be empowering; it is up to the researchers to ensure that it is so (Everitt *et al.*, 1992; Humphries, 1996); and
- User research provides one of the most effective tools for empowering research.

Thus *power* emerges as a key issue within user research. User research has been developed as a method of creating new knowledge, hitherto hidden and often described as invalid by professionals. Knowledge itself is powerful in providing a way to make sense, give meaning and predict reality. In addition, it has the potential to lead to a shift in the existing knowledge established by professionals, by offering a new way of looking at what been taken for granted by them, often offering an alternative critical perspective. Thus it can be a powerful tool with which to challenge professional knowledge.

Gaining the ability to carry out research, either alongside professional researchers or on par with them, is adding competencies, and conferring a socially desirable status on service users as they undertake a socially valued role, all of which empower them to achieve equality in power with non-labelled citizens.

Power is also an issue in paying users for their work in research, as payment symbolises recognition for socially valued work – in this case paying people where the majority would be living on benefits and hence be poor. That the pay has to fit the limits put on earnings for those claiming benefits is not an issue that can be resolved easily (see Chapters 6, 7 and 11). Pay has to be thought through in advance, including the waiting time between carrying out a research task and being paid for it.

Thus a number of positive aspects of power come to the fore in user research, so unlike the experience of being service user, largely overburdened by the negative connotation of power. Power is also an issue in taking into account the context of user research, where age, class, ethnicity and gender play a part in determining who is likely to become (and remain) a service user, as well as in whether specific types of intervention will be a help or a hindrance to users (see Chapters 4 and 5).

Finally, power is an issue in the relationships between user-researchers and professional researchers when the aim is collaborative work. As the professional researcher usually comes with greater knowledge and skills in the research process, and the user-researcher comes with considerable experiential knowledge, the risk of the former controlling the latter should not be underestimated, as methodological knowledge and skills continue to be essential for building up the ability of users to be researchers. Often, users arrive lacking in confidence about their abilities to do research, as well as doubts as to the usefulness of engaging in anything using complicated jargon and portrayed as 'academic', while also being attracted to it. Some come with a niggling suspicion why professional researchers would wish to work with them, if not to exploit their experience in order to glorify the professional researcher.

Professional researchers may come with a sense of superiority and confidence, either unsure whether users can master the skills required to meet the research tasks, or expecting them to be as good as the professionals very quickly. The niggling doubts and low self-esteem of many highly intelligent users, at times manifesting in a reluctance to take decisions or taking 'too much' time over it, comes as an unwelcome surprise to professional researchers.

Not coming from the research world, users may not appreciate that most professional researchers keen to work with users in partnership are to an extent risking their credibility as researchers in the eyes of the majority of the colleagues. They are also demonstrating readiness to take a risk by opting for a much less chartered route of research, working with non-professional researchers, and the ups and downs of a participatory path.

Given the funding structure, often the funding will be given to the professional researcher to be responsible for, accentuating the sense of the latter being more powerful than the user researcher. In extreme situations, this may feel like a clash of two cultures. In less extreme instances it is about taking pains to learn about, and from, each other within a framework that is structured to be user-led from the very beginning. The Joseph Rowntree Foundation recently announced that its disability research sector will be guided by a user group coming out of the 'Shaping Our Lives' social care project; it is hoped that this is an attempt to ensure the research agenda is more user-led.

This scenario has led a number of users not wishing to engage in research, or to wanting to do it on their own, either by hiring a 'tame' researcher to act as a consultant, or by attempting to 'reinvent the wheel' of research. Yet, in my view, all three are missed opportunities, as each partner has a lot to offer the other.

It is crucial that user-led research is of good quality, given that:

i. Poor quality research is not worth investing in if the aim is ultimately to contribute to improving users' lives; and ii The expectation that user research will fail and will be exposed as poor research by a large number of those who doubt the validity of involving such researchers in the first place.

High-quality user research needs good professional knowledge of research as much as the experiential knowledge brought in by the users.

As the definition of being a user is wide-ranging and subjective, and a number of the professional researchers may have been service users intermittently, we are treading in 'muddy waters' here when arguing that people who are not defining themselves as users cannot be valued contributors to user-led research. The multiplicity of identities ascribed to the authors of this book, typical of postmodernity, also highlights this point.

Hence, within the collaborative relationships, it is necessary to find ways that enable not only the coexistence of users and professional researchers, but also the genuine participation of both as equal contributors in a shared endeavour. This is possible, if not always comfortable, or easy. For example, in the Lifecraft (a user-led Cambridge based organisation) evaluation (Barrett *et al.*, 1999) the users participated in interviewing the research adviser; with her they spent time learning to understand the logic of research in a demystified format, proceeding to formulate the research questions, and later the method, as well as carrying out the study to its completion. This was not carried out in equal measures by all of them. The research adviser worked on some components much more than others, while the user-researchers contributed more to other elements. The project manager and the director of Lifecraft were involved with it directly at the beginning and at the end, but only indirectly throughout most of the time during which it evolved.

I admit to being weary of highly formalised procedures with which to anchor good partnerships between user-researchers and professional researchers, as these can become too rigid and are never going to encapsulate all eventualities, while seeing the need for an agreed framework from which to work on the partnership itself. In principle, there is also a place for non-users to research users, as much as for users to research non-users, if multi-perspectives are the objective (Harris and Paylor, 1999). However, this aspect is not the focus of this book.

User research is thus defined here as one in which users are equal partners regarding the major decisions taken about the research and the whole research process, with the research focus being driven by users' concerns. This operational definition differs from the more formal 'user-controlled' (Beresford and Wallcraft, 1997; Evans and Fisher, 1998), and takes its cue from the concept of 'Prosumers', coined by Monica Savio (Savio, 2000) in her attempt to describe and analyse the role of users in a welfare organisation, in which they are producers of relationships, interactions, outcomes and processes, as much as consumers of these parameters produced by others, such as practitioners, professional researchers and research participants.

Representation

As Purtell, Baxter and Mitchell write in this volume (see Chapter 11), they are questioned accusatorily as to whether the users interested in research do indeed represent all users in an area, or of a particular disability. This is unlikely to be the case, as people interested in research, let alone those who become engaged in it, tend to be a minority in the population which credits systematic investigation as having more meaning than sporadic individual experiences. It is unclear why user-researchers are expected to be more representative of either users or researchers than researchers are generally.

However, there is a clear need to ensure the best available representation of the diversity of the population studied in any research about people, groups and populations, for the purpose of being able to reach more generalisable meanings and (at times) recommendations.

Ethical committees

Ethical committees have a difficult task on their hands. They need to ensure that research participants will not be harmed as a result of research, that they will be respected; and that the information they provide will be treated ethically too. Equally, they have to satisfy themselves that the research is of good quality and will be carried out in good faith. As user research is largely uncharted territory for these committees, it is understandable that they would wish to be extra vigilant regarding the ethical conduct of user-led projects.

However, it would be rare at present to find among the members of the committees people with previous experience of user research, knowledge about it, or commitment to it. At best, a committee will be sufficiently assured that the researchers know what research is about, and have observed ethical principles before. Fear of the loss of professional authority and power, stereotypical ideas about users – especially those with mental ill-health – are invariably bound to come to the fore.

> The three of us enter the room, to be confronted by a group of about ten people, none known to us, and of whom only one – the chair – introduces himself. We get to know who some of them are when they speak. They are all professionals, mostly doctors, all from the NHS; there are no representatives of social services, the voluntary sector, service
>
> ▶

◀

users, or carers. We learn in the process that one of them represents the lay public: she happens to be a nurse by training.

One of us is a user of mental health services who is also a professional researcher; the two others are professional researchers who have been in psychotherapy, but are not known as service users. None of us works for the trust the committee represents.

A number of the comments and questions are pertinent, pointing to the need to secure consistency of terminology and procedure, as well as the affirmation of consent by potential research participants.

Some of the comments and questions make us wonder how far apart we and the committee are in understanding what research with users is about. For example:

● We are told that user researchers, volunteering to undertake the training and screened by us, need to get the permission of their care manager and GP prior to commencing the training;

● Ward managers are not perceived as good enough figures to pass judgement as to whether a specific patient will be asked if s/he wishes to participate in the research by a number of those present. They are unhappy that we have omitted to give this responsibility to the consultant. After what feels like a very long time, a compromise is reached, in that the ward manager needs to consult the clinical team prior to making the decision.

● We are asked if we – the professional researchers – would be present at every interview carried out by user-researchers, in case 'they become manic'. Luckily someone in the room reminds the members that this would miss the purpose of involving users as researchers, and we are able to indicate our safety net approach in which user-researchers who are unwell have to inform us as soon as possible and we get in touch with the participants to postpone the meeting, or to re-arrange it with someone else if needed.

● We are not asked even one question about the training we wish to offer, or the content of the encounter we wish to have with users participants.

As we left the room we understood that, given the power relationships, we either follow the wishes of the committee or give up the project. We were left with a number of ethical dilemmas, among them how to justify to the user-researchers the procedure recommended by the committee for their own involvement in the research.

Unless these committees contain representatives of user-researchers and of researchers using interpretative approaches it is difficult to see how they will become better informed, and hence better equipped to reach sensible decisions concerning user research.

Ethical committees thus represent an instance within the research process in which the opening up in research perspectives is largely yet to happen, while greater tolerance of unconventional approaches to research can be discerned. User-researchers would need to be well prepared and well supported for their encounters with ethical committees; partnership with local agencies would help too.

Training

Can the research be of high quality if the researchers are not qualified? Most of the contributions to this book demonstrate that it is possible to carry out high quality research when not all, or even most, of the researchers have had research experience. A crucial factor in leading to the success or failure of user research projects is the training on offer.

This training has to achieve seemingly paradoxical objectives. It has to demystify research and 'dejargonise' its language, on the one hand, while enabling people to have a good enough understanding of the internal logic of research and its application to the issues investigated, on the other. It also has to inspire participants to the point that they wish to remain throughout the whole process, which inevitably has some less interesting or/and uncomfortable elements. While they may not possess research skills at the outset, they should be encouraged to contribute actively from their considerable experience, and with the relevant generic skills they often bring, such as being good listeners, respectful and able to demonstrate empathy. Trainees need to feel early on that they are making progress individually and as a group, be supported when stuck, and praised for their achievements. How to enable participants not to be interviewed if they change their minds or are flooded by the impact of past experiences is an important skill to be practised side by side with debriefing techniques for the user-researchers themselves. Lots of experiential opportunities; realistic role play, experimenting with being in the shoes or unde the skin of others; and learning from other user-researchers are essential.

The training is thus a central stage of the research, in which decisions are reached and implemented regarding the research questions and methodology.

The training period can, and should be, used for confidence- and trust-building, for providing detailed and accurate information about the various aspects of the research, including payment for the work, and for raising doubts and questions. In short, all the principles of adult learning, now redis-covered on many nursing and social work qualifying courses, apply to this case too. Chapters 4, 6 and 7 offer relevant examples.

In contrast, Avril Butler (Chapter 3) and Reima Maglijlic (Chapter 9) took the position that clear ground rules would suffice. This was possible in the context of their projects, where the participants did not have to reach out to others, but acted as both co-researchers and research participants.

The training process also provides a 'cooling-off' period in which users who find that this is not what they wish to – or can effectively – do, are able to leave without losing face. It is trickier – and requires considerable tact – for the training co-ordinators to encourage some unsuitable users to leave, yet it may be necessary instead of setting them to fail, and/or letting them fail the research participants.

The inclusion of practitioners as active research partners also needs a training element. Most existing joint user–professional research organisers have not attempted to train the professional contributors. This is an omission, waiting to be put right, for there is little in the experience of professional researchers to prepare them for this type of equal participation. It would be best carried out by user-researchers and those professional researchers already taking part in this type of research.

Support structures throughout the lifetime of the research project
These are as relevant to the training phase as at any stage of the research project. Effective support is essential as users are at times vulnerable because of personal crises, or through issues with which the research may confront them. Group interaction may also lead to conflict from time to time, most of which can be resolved by good informal support provided by someone the users know and trust. Accessibility is essential too.

Dissemination
The importance of this phase of research is emphasised more today than used to be the case, in recognition of the alarming lack of knowledge about relevant, specific research projects and the application of their findings by agencies that should know better, by practitioners, and at times by policy-makers. Indeed, what is the point of investing in research if lessons are not learned from it?

Attempting to remedy this sorry state of affairs, the reasons for which have been outlined in the introduction to this book, the government, urged by the National Institute of Social Work (NISW) has established 'Social Care for Information Excellence' (SCIE) as a disseminating body for social care, while NICE has similar, and additional, responsibilities for health care. As already mentioned, NICE is expected to determine the value of research and of specific interventions, such as medication.

Presumably, the government accepts that existing social care evidence is not of a calibre sufficient to enable this type of judgement to be passed. Those sceptical of the validity of the type of evidence favoured by NICE – invariably of a positivistic origin – would argue that this belief needs to be extended to the health sphere too. Most current user research would only merit consideration as 'grey' evidence, terminology used in official publications of research bids by the Department of Health as inferior in quality to research carried out without the active participation of users.

At the same time, the emphasis on much wider dissemination of research in both health and social care should be welcomed, as it has the potential to open up this hitherto neglected area to all those frontline workers and managers, users and carers, thus far uninitiated into the appreciation and use of research, let alone participating in conducting it.

The NHS also initiated 'Consumers in NHS Research' in 1999, which is to include also, from 2002, social care. This organisation focuses on informing users – and anyone else on the mailing list – of research activities focused on user issues, via a newsletter and workshops. Thus far, the information provided has depended on information received from those who have answered the longish questionnaire the organisation sends out by post. The systematic provision of knowledge, skills and debate on problematic issues in research for users is still not happening. The organisation has just been merged with the Cancer Development Network and has allied itself with the social care research arm of York University. Are these signs of a better, more inclusive, future for user research? Or perhaps for a narrower one, in both terms of category of disability and research framework? Only time will tell.

The Toronto group aims at promoting empowering research in health and social care. It is a national group of mainly social care researchers and users interested in research. The Mental Health Foundation has established a network of user-researchers in this field, based on its activities. It prefers a user-only model.

The research network described by Purtell, Baxter and Mitchell (see Chapter 11), and the one initiated by the department of social work at Birmingham University, are examples of regional and local networks.

If anything, these recent developments accentuate the urgent need to disseminate user research to all stakeholder groups, beginning with other users, but aiming also to reach carers, practitioners, managers, researchers, policy-makers and politicians. Chapters 3, 4, 5 and 8 illustrate some of the ways in which this can be achieved. It is important for user-researchers to have the skills required for dissemination, such as public speaking, writing and/or the use of multimedia methods, as well as in-built opportunities for doing so within each project, be it at local, regional, national or international level. Paying for the expenses incurred by dissemination (for example, travelling expenses, work on preparing a newsletter, a CD-Rom) needs to be taken care of in advance to ensure the involvement of user-researchers in dissemination. In addition to spreading information about a specific project and its message, the engagement in dissemination offers opportunities for further learning for the user-researcher, engaging in a dialogue with other stakeholders to research, greater awareness of what has an impact on research, and networking.

This chapter opened with an illustration of the powerful impact of local dissemination. That it came as a surprise to all of those engaged in the research project reflects our naïvety as to the impact of user research. When this project was presented to other audiences it was to great acclaim, and elicited many comments and questions.

What do user-researchers do when the project in which they have participated finishes?

This phase may feel like an anticlimax, or like being abandoned. Networking in advance can prevent this from happening, or perhaps laying of a foundation for further joint activity stemming from the project, such as a further dissemination step in the near future.

For some user-researchers participation in a research project provides the incentive to engage in further studies, either about research or around other issues. Others may move in the direction of becoming more active around user issues. Most user-researchers, but not all, comment on the positive sense of achievement in mastering the research task, in communicating with the research participants, in informing professionals about vital yet hitherto missing aspects of user experience, and in making professionals listen respectfully to users. All of these highlight the social role-valorisation aspect of this activity, its empowering value, and its place in destigmatising service users.

The capacity building, the enhancement of human and social capital that are embedded in enabling users to act as researchers could – and should – be utilised further by health and social care agencies in their locality in building a network of user–researchers, for employment in future projects. The same applies to the contribution to professional knowledge brought about by user research.

References

Barnes, C and Mercer, G (eds) (1997) *Doing Disability Research* Leeds, Disability Press

Barnes, M and Bowl, R (2001) *Taking Over the Asylum: Empowerment and Mental Health* Basingstoke, Palgrave

Barrett, M, Morgan, C, Knight, T, Smith, S and Maglajlic, R (1999) *Lifecraft Evaluation* Cambridge, Anglia Polytechnic University

Barry, M and Hallett, C (eds) (1998) *Social Exclusion and Social Work: Issues of Theory, Policy and Practice* Lyme Regis, Russell House

Beresford, P and Wallcraft, J (1997) 'Psychiatric system survivors and emancipatory research: issues, overlaps and differences' in: Barnes, C and Mercer, G (eds) *Doing Disability Research* Leeds, the Disability Press, pp 65–87

Chahal, K (1999) 'Researching ethnicity: Experiences and concerns' in: Broad, B (ed.) *The Politics of Social Work Research and Evaluation*, Birmingham, Venture Press, pp 59–75

Campbell, D (1963) *Experimental and Quasi-experimental Designs for Research* Chicago, IL, Rand McNally

Evans, C and Fisher, M (1998) 'User controlled research and empowerment' in: Shera, W and Wells, L (eds) *Empowerment Practice in Social Work: Developing Richer Conceptual Foundations* Toronto, Canadian Scholars Press, pp 348–69

Everitt, A, Hardiker, P, Littlewood, J and Mullender, A (1992) *Applied Research for Better Practice* London, Macmillan

Fawcett, B, Featherstone, B Fook, J and Rossiter, A (eds) (2000) *Practice + Research in Social Work: Postmodern feminist perspectives* London Routledge

Harris, J and Paylor, I (1999) 'The Politics of difference: Researching those dissimilar from the self' in: Broad, B (ed.) *The Politics of Social Work Research and evaluation* Birmingham, Venture Press, pp 31–44

Hughes, J (1990) *The Philosophy of Social Research* London, Longman

Humphries, B (ed.) (1996) *Critical Perspectives on Empowerment* Birmingham, Venture Press

Kuhn, T (1970) *The Structure of Scientific Revolutions* (2nd edn) Chicago, IL, University of Chicago Press

Macdonald, G M and Sheldon, B (1992) 'Contemporary studies of the effectiveness of social work' *British Journal of Social Work*, 22 (6) pp 615–43

Oliver, M (1992) 'Changing the social relations of research production?' *Disability, Handicap & Society* 7 (2) 101–13

Oliver, M (1996) *Understanding Disability: From theory to practice* London, Macmillan

Popper, K (1941) *The Logic of Scientific Discovery* London, Heinmann

Savio, M (2000) 'The dynamics of management', Unpublished paper, Moscow and Irkustk, Tempus Programme Health Management of Russian Children and Maternity Services

Strauss, A and Corbin, J (1990) *Basics of Qualitative Research: Grounded theory procedures and techniques* London, Sage

Swain, J, Finklestein, V, French, S and Oliver, M (eds) (1993) *Disabling Barriers–Enabling Environments* London, Sage

Taylor, R Thornicroft, G (1996) 'Uses and limits of randomised controlled trials in mental health service research' in: Tansella, M and Thornicroft, G (eds) *Mental Health Outcomes Measures* Berlin, Springer, pp 144–51

Thyer, B (1993) 'Social work theory and practice research: An approach of logical positivism' *Social Work and Social Science Review*, 4 (1) 5–26

Winter, R and Munn-Giddings, C (2001) *A handbook for Action Research in Health and Social Care* London, Routledge

CHAPTER 2
Researching Oneself through Reflective Writing
Joanna Payne

This chapter is a personal account of the researcher researching herself and finding ways to reconcile her own experience of a mental health problem with those of the client group with which she works.

To begin the process, I undertook a modular distance-learning programme called 'Reflective Writing for Professional Learning'. Our group was made up of four mental health professionals: one from health, one from social services, a university professor and myself (there were two others, but they dropped out after the first two sessions). The intention of the course was to explore how we could improve our understanding and expertise through writing reflectively in a way that could communicate effectively and sensitively our reactions to professional experience.

This process of reflection affected my colleagues and I in ways we could not have anticipated in advance: a journey of discovery for me – unexpected, in some ways quite harrowing, and challenging in every way. My initial intentions were to explore issues that were not related to me personally, but rather that would improve my practice. I found myself writing about my experiences of twelve years as a schizophrenia survivor, synthesising and processing these experiences both to enable other people and to empower myself.

The role of reflection
Reflection in practice is a way of improving and developing one's own skills. Reflection is about thinking differently and laterally; exploring implications in one's own actions and relationships with other people; discovering different areas through reading, thinking and looking at practice. This process of reflective practice is summed up accurately by Winter *et al.*, (1999) quoting from Schoen (1983, p. 50), as:

> The 'artistry' of reflective practice, says Donald Schoen, refers to the close link between expert action and understanding which occurs whenever we deal sensitively and effectively with 'situations of uncertainty, instability, uniqueness and value-conflict' (Schoen 183: p.50). In other words, 'artistry' is required on all those many occasions when there is no simple general rule, no simple right way of doing things.
> (Winter *et al.*, 1999, p. 2)

Winter *et al.*, begin to explore the way people reflect through different kinds of writing: how the process of writing can encourage individuals to reflect and engage in a safe way which they usually may not be able to. Winter (1999:1) expresses the meaning of writing fiction based upon the Latin word *fingere* meaning 'to shape, to fashion, to mould'. They continue:

> *So writing 'fictions' ... refers generally to the process of exploring and reflecting on the meanings of experience by representing it in forms of writing which have been shaped by the writer's imagination. By 'imag- ination' we don't just mean general mental agility and resourcefulness; we mean specifically the creative faculty which shapes the raw material of experience in **artistic** form.* (ibid: 1)

By means of fiction, 'faction' (a term used within our small discussion group to refer to a process of writing fiction that is based on fact) and reflec- tive writing we can begin to draw out themes, explore things we were not previously aware of, and begin to discover what we think and feel about our professional practice.

The reflective writing process

We produced work every fortnight and met to discuss our masterpieces. Everyone was anxious and uncertain during the first meeting – discussion was stilted and it was difficult to communicate safely about thoughts in our heads and hearts. But soon we began to come together as people who respected and supported each other through the process. I wrote as a service user – the first time I had decided to be so honest about my own experiences.

The researcher began to research herself through her own writing, coming to terms with a horror she had never really faced. The reflective writing I had always enjoyed as a teenager disappeared at the age of nineteen with the onset of schizophrenia. Writing and self-expression became too painful, too frightening, too terrible. Thoughts too bizarre to express to anyone were written down to be discovered with embarrassment, pain an disbelief when read later. Writing stopped for ten years. However, an M.A. module gave the legitimacy and freedom to write.

I had started a new job working with mental health carers – the first time I had begun to work with this group, people with first-hand experience of the suffering caused by mental illness. Reflective writing developed my own ability to express my experiences of mental illness, to assist and complement my practice and legitimise my experiences.

This process was not always easy and represented a complex and difficult choice of 'coming out as a service user'. My reflective diary shows a time when I explore these issues with a sense of bewilderment and anxiety:

> *There is stigma for those who do not succeed, do not turn their experiences to positive effect.*

Stigma, stigma, where art thou? Are thou leaning out of the balcony looking at me, or are you shut inside the door? You will never live a normal life. I am sorry for you! Wait! Watch and hope! No belief that anyone will ever discriminate, no belief that anyone will understand.
(Reflective Diary, 23 October).

The 'thought creations'

We developed 'thought creations'. I use this term to describe loosely the work each one of us produced. We were given the freedom to write under-pinned by a legitimacy supplied by the title 'MA module' that recognised its relevance and value. We were also led and guided by each other as a group of people who would never have found the time to come together without the justification of certificated study.

The best way I can begin to describe the process is by presenting a number of examples of the work we discussed together. The two pieces I present are clearly linked. The linking themes of 'betrayal', 'blessings' and 'burn out' feature very strongly in both examples. The writing of the second piece arose from a discussion with colleagues, who began to understand the thoughts and feelings swimming in my head much better than I could. The first is a moving account of one of the consultation meetings with a group of carers.

We have heard it all before; our final betrayal – and – from one of us!

The brief

My job is to consult carers. To listen to carers. Engage with people and carry out a consultation process. I facilitate the meetings. Promising people we will listen. This is part of the Blair Government's commitment to user and carer consultation. A commitment to user and carer involvement. The *Local Implementation Plan* (LIP) and *Local Carers' Strategy Plan. A National Service Framework for Mental Health. Caring About Carers, Standard 6* (1999, p. 72). Putting mental health at the forefront of development and resources.

The background and the blessings we offer

We sit in my territory, where a group gathers to discuss their problems. It is a support group for them, to air their views, to express their opinions. We sit in a Carers' Centre, where carers are empowered, supported, blessed with our attention. They come from a chaotic, anxious, frustrating world which is their home. They are real carers in the true meaning of the word. *A carer who provides care for a person to help them stay well, to support them ... This is our time.*

The betrayal for carers

We have come to consult you ... We have this document outlining the fact that you have a say ... The management board is accountable to you ... This government tries to be transparent, accountable ... to listen to you. I believe ... *We know you have come to do a job, it's just a job to you. It affects our lives, we have heard it all before. We are disillusioned...*

My personal brief

God – what can I do? I believe in what I am doing. All these documents espousing user consultation, public accountability, transparency, recognition of your role as a carer ... *I recognise this and I see your role. But do they? Those that have the power, sit on the board, never have contact.*

My background

I experience a similar disillusionment, and sadness. I am attacked for what *they* do and don't do. What can I, the I, the *ego* do? I ask myself – can I justify my own existence? *The money for your consultation could provide a service for our son, daughter – the person I care for.*

Their belief

Who am I to say we can offer this service? This consultation – what is it? Is it a paper exercise with limited and ever-shrinking resources? *They promised. Always promised ... They held a meeting ... Got us all together and we went through all this before. What can you do?*

My background which is no longer a betrayal.

I can bring sincerity. I can bring my personal experience as a service user who can work. Not the slick talker who justifies the management board commission. What can I do? A job or a personal commitment? Am I any different?

I ask a friend who expresses sadness. Makes me think beyond my own world of middle-class egotism, yet at the same time a living hell (or hell of a survival trick with a diagnosis of schizophrenia) made easier by middle-class comfort and complacency. A mixture of great knowledge, yet exclusion through an ability to articulate, to live in comfort, to be educated and able to express myself. Am I part of them, or part of *them in power that do and say and direct*? A dichotomy and a paradox. Who am I and who do I represent? Examine my own values.

His background, betrayal and burnout

I am *me* with all I bring and all I take. I am surrounded by incredible people. I have seen a homeless man – an amazing man driven to complete disillusionment by the group he represented of homeless people not supporting him. Not their apathy, but their inability 'to engage in the system' – maybe too ill and disillusioned themselves to operate. I have seen others, driven down. Yet what can I do in this culture of apathy. I can only bring me and be me. I can only bring myself, but what I can achieve through that I do not know – maybe nothing, maybe everything, maybe mediocrity. But I will try!

Their betrayal, and their belief

Health Improvement Plans ... more money than the last government. *Joint Investment Plans* producing joint working between agencies. National Service Frameworks emphasising the importance of mental health. *We have heard it all before. Where do the resources come from? The money to do this project could fund this? Not enough CPNs (community psychiatric nurses), or social workers?*

The final betrayal that beggars belief

Christopher Clunis ... Zito ... The latest suicide. Reality? *A question.* Reality! *A statement.* Resources! *A reality?!? Very few people who are Schizophrenia sufferers do as well as you. They suffer you know and we suffer you know. What drives a carer to ask for their son or daughter to be sectioned ... Their son to be removed for their own well-being. What does that do to our relationship? We betrayed them! And now you ask us what we want? Can I believe? Dare to hope? Or will you betray me as well?*

My blessings to you contained in a letter to a friend.
I cannot betray. Can I bless?

Dear Friend, I know you were quite sad on the phone when I spoke about the 'consultation exercise' late Thursday night. I don't know if you have any suggestions of what I can do.

You told me quite a few years ago to try to make every conversation a pleasure for the other person to listen to, and treat every circumstance as a learning opportunity for both. I don't know anything else, or power that I have to actually influence things. I can see this being a consultation exercise, I have also heard the crap about heightening people's expectations. I hope there will be funding to actually develop the services, which is something I hope to do – to implement changes! Your talking tells me that my role as a service user and professional will merge and grow together to bring better service/experiences with which I can bless people I meet, with people who are connected to mental health service users. My Brief, my Blessing – my Burnout, my Background, my final Betrayal?!?

Just a couple of thoughts!

All the best ...

The next account arises from a description of the experiences of one colleague who I have had the privilege of knowing. From my own personal experiences of distress, I share the same feelings of uncertainty and fear of burnout.

Did he nearly make it? And the possibilities!

He had a rather drawn, white face – hair rather dishevelled, always looked a little withdrawn, remote in the way he engaged with the world. He had a passion. He was completely impassioned in supporting the homeless people he represented. This was a world he had come from, he knew this world. He had been a drunk for sixteen years. Slept under bridges, in doorways, in shop windows. It was the world he knew and the world he could represent more than anyone else. He had come to this place, this hostel and 'been saved' – both in the meaning of rescued from his drunkenness, and saved and born again with a quiet faith in God. He always dressed in a dishevelled manner, never quite 'making the transition to the smart casual look of the work world'. His clothes always slightly on the big side, hanging off rangy arms which were rather thin, all under that slightly dishevelled hair and that white face which made him look perpetually tired, perpetually ill and slightly under-nourished. He, however, had made it.

He had moved out from the streets. He had moved into the hostel. He had moved into his own home. He had started to operate in the world of ordinary rents, jobs, buying food, managing bills. He had made it. But he hadn't forgotten those he had once known who slept on the streets, in the doorways, in the shop windows reflecting money and affluence contrasted with the poverty of those separated by a thin, transparent pane of glass — nothing separating them except the impenetrable glass. He had not forgotten. He worked with schools, with the hostel, with the power he now owned.

He told stories of 'never run away from home' to school children. 'London is not the centre of the world. Try to work it out.' He met with his friends in the hostel. He met with councillors, the user representative on the committees. He was it. He knew. He could speak with passion about the experiences. His oft-repeated mantra: 'Your feet are cold. You are freezing. Someone offers you a drink. You take a swig. You feel better. Drink numbs the feet, numbs the cold. You then begin to drink. I drank for sixteen years....' He is a part of this group. But somehow now he doesn't quite connect, quite relate to people. He is projected into a position of power. Is he one of them? Or one of us, they wonder! He sits on the committees. He represents. He has power!

He organises a big meeting. Everyone will be there! Staff, but most importantly the homeless people he represents. He goes around asking them to attend. There are banners made; catering organised; a big buffet of food. It is all there in place. They will attend - it is for them.

The meeting is ready. It is raining slightly outside. Many people are expected. It is 10 a.m. The staff representatives of organisations assemble. His face begins to show signs of worry. Where are they? The homeless people this is for? It is 10.25. They are not coming? Where are they? He goes outside and his face is broken. His face and being crumbles. He is broken. He speaks in his rather dramatic, rather driving shout. He goes through the motions of telling so many about it. About their rights – the homeless people are not there.

You have done a good job ... We owe you ... We will make sure more people come next time ... Publicise it ... They are not here!

He looks a broken man!

Two weeks later he leaves for London. He is no longer there. Where is he? His enthusiasm? His energy? His betrayal!

Conclusion

The opportunity to research myself was a unique journey of self-discovery aided by colleagues within the group, who were able to draw hidden issues to the fore. Research about oneself cannot be expressed through words safely hidden behind other identities expressed 'about' other research participants. It is about oneself. My colleagues were surprised at my honesty and commented on the insight they found in the words. I ask the question: why were people surprised? I find myself reading autobiographies of equal honesty and directness. I think of the recent book about his cancer by John Diamond (Diamond, 2000) and the direct honesty of his words. Why can cancer be discussed without stigma in a newspaper column and yet the admission of schizophrenia be surprising? The acclaimed novel, *The Noonday Demon* (Solomon, 2001) focusing on the harrowing experiences of people who have depression, shares this goal. Solomon writes:

> *I have asked my subjects to allow me to use their actual names,*
> *because real names lend authority to real stories. In a book one of the*
> *aims of which is to remove the burden of stigma from mental illness, it*
> *is important not to play to that stigma by hiding the identities of*
> *depressed people.* (p. 11)

There is a danger in coming out as a schizophrenia survivor, meeting prejudices from people who do not understand. How safe am I to share it?

- *The dilemma*: Will I prejudice people against me?
- *The opportunity*: I can help people to understand and comprehend mental illness and health.

- *The surprise*: Mental health professionals can begin to understand.
- *The outcome*: I am no longer afraid and I am a service user and professional who does not betray, but blesses – even if she fears burnout!

References

Department of Health (1995) *Carers' Recognition and Services Act* London, HMSO

Department of Health (1999a) *A National Framework for Mental Health Modern Standards and Service Models Standard 6: Caring About Carers* London, HMSO, p. 72

Department of Health (1999b) *Caring About Carers: A National Strategy for Carers* London, HMSO, pp 12–3

Diamond, J (1998) *C Because Cowards get Cancer too...* London, Vermilion

Schoen, D (1983) *The Reflective Practitioner,*New York, Basic Books, p 50

Solomon, A (2001) *The Noonday Demon An anatomy of depression* London, Chatto & Windus

Winter, R, Buck, A and Sobiechowska, P, (1999) *Professional Experience and the Investigative Imagination: The ART of reflective writing* London, Routledge, p 2

CHAPTER 3
Whose Life is it Anyway?
creative autobiography with service users

Avril Butler

Autobiographical competence – the capacity and confidence to compose one's own story – is central to psychic health (West, 2001, p.31)

This chapter is an exploration of some of the principles of inclusive research drawn from my work with a group of women at a small non-government family centre. It includes consideration of the various meanings of 'research' in this situation, and of the instability of the notion of 'service user involvement'. It defines inclusive research as that which is with, by and for service users rather than 'on' them. The origins and context for the group are explained, and information about the technique used and key elements of creative autobiography groupwork is given. Some illustration of the metaphors chosen and their impact provide the basis for reflection on power relationships and ethical issues. In the concluding section, attention is given to the principles which are transferable to other forms of research and practice activity.

Origins and context
There is substantial current interest in narrative and biographical methods in all aspects of the 'helping professions' (Chamberlayne *et al.*, 2000) driven by the essentially partial nature of scientific knowledge in informing work with people. Evidence of this is to be found in psychology and dementia care (Bender and Cheston, 1999), in medical practice (Greenhalgh and Hurwitz, 1999; West, 2000), and as a long-established tradition in social and community work (Martin, 1995; Laird, 1994; White and Epston, 1990). Much of the work focuses on text and analysis of meaning while acknowledging the important distinction between reporting and reconstructing life narratives. For people experiencing social and medical distress, the capacity to express their experience and to reintegrate the different aspects of this experience into a coherent life story, may be as important as alleviation of the presenting problem. In an early work on feminist methodology, Maria Mies (1983) cites a study of women's individual and social history as a precursor to, and foundation for, active participation and political involvement.

The subject of this chapter is a 'life-story project' carried out by a group of six women staff[1] and users of a resource for children and families in a deprived inner-city neighbourhood. The group met over a six-month period and used creative autobiography to explore participants' lives. Follow-up interviews were conducted after the group, and some of the findings inform this chapter. The origins of the work lay in the women's interest in mental health issues and a wish to explore lives and identities in ways that did not pathologise.

Creative autobiography

This is a groupwork technique I developed in 1993. The basis of the technique is to provide a structure within which participants can explore and recreate their own life stories in unconventional ways, using self-chosen creative metaphors (Butler, 2000). Participants do not need either writing skills or 'artistic' ability to make use of the process, as the emphasis is on learning to look at lives in a different way, revisit memories and make sense of things for themselves. This is particularly useful for people who lack emotional fluency or who are not articulate or confident in forms of self-expression. The method avoids the use of written chronological accounts because of the way language and meaning tend to be socially constructed and limiting. The method also promotes confidence in self-as-expert and is directed primarily at self-as-audience. Group members are encouraged to identify a project or metaphor to represent an aspect of their lives. In developing and exploring the meaning of these metaphors, participants engage in a form of auto-ethnography (Saukko, 1995). Individuals use the group sessions to refine the ideas they have, and to become clearer about the meaning they attach to the project. Group members have opportunities to ask questions and respond to what is brought up, but not to analyse or take responsibility for other people's feelings.

As a long-term agency management group member, I was known, to some degree, to all the women, and for my work in women's mental health groups. As a group of women, we shared experiences of motherhood, being white, British, and a connection with the agency. We had very different experiences of age, educational background, sexual orientation, familiarity with group processes, emotional fluency, and access to power and privilege. The women's research agenda was concerned with the meaning of their own life stories and experiences within a context of mental health understanding. All had experienced some degree of emotional distress and wanted to know more about it. As a participant in the group, I shared this agenda and additionally wanted to explore the impact of creative autobiography as a technique.

Beginnings

Initial work was concerned with creating a context that would facilitate exploration and sharing. There is some debate about the validity of narrative in research. Linden West's study exploring the interface of personal and professional identities of inner-city GPs deals well with what he describes as 'imagining the real', in which research is conceived to be 'a collaborative act of the imagination as much as of the intellect, of feeling as well as thought; a shared empathic recreation and reinterpretation of experience' (West, 2001, p. 13). The important factors in the life-story group were that group members would be able to create new narratives for themselves without feeling constrained by convention. In response to the expressed interest in mental health by the women of the project, both staff and users were invited to an open session at which I offered an exhibition representing my critical autobiography[2] (Griffiths, 1995) of mental ill-health as a catalyst for discussion.

Important preliminary elements

- *Initiation and motivation*: The work was a response to an approach by women at the centre and did not originate with me as a researcher;
- *Personal exposure*: As the facilitator/researcher and person with substantial power I offered my own vulnerability as a starting point;
- *Multiple media*: Alongside a written invitation and verbal explanation, there were pictures and collages to stimulate responses and to give examples of creative autobiography; and
- *Challenging dominant discourse*: Mental health was presented as a continuum rather than a dichotomy to encourage women to acknowledge fluctuations as being normal.

Women were offered the opportunity to participate in a group to focus on their own lives. A simple, written invitation to join a life-story group was circulated to all the women in the project, and they were encouraged to ask questions. An initial information session was offered, and used to clarify expectations and reach agreements about the way the group would operate. A closed, time-limited group was agreed and careful attention given to setting ground-rules based on confidentiality, support, participation and self-responsibility. These are set out below and convey how the group ran.

Ground-rules
Confidentiality means:

- Not gossiping;
- Being able to talk about the group without identifying individuals;
- Not using anything from the group in a way that would hurt anybody; and
- Any writing about the work will use fictitious names, and the autobiographical work will only be included in academic writing if individuals want it to be.

Support means:

- Sharing things from our experiences which may feel very tentative and vulnerable;
- Encouraging others to express more accurately what they are feeling;

- Absolutely not giving explanations or interpretations of other people's feelings or behaviour; and
- Validating each other's experience: if we do not understand we will acknowledge and try to understand more, not dismiss.

Participation means:
- Being at the group and contributing at whatever level and amount feels right. It does not mean everyone doing the same thing;
- If low participation of another group member becomes uncomfortable for someone, they will say so; and
- If high participation means someone feels there is not enough time for them, they will say so.

Self-responsibility means:
- Individuals retain responsibility for their own work and any feelings or consequences of group membership. What to share, and how much, is always in the control of the individual;
- Group members will leave space for strong feelings of any kind and will not try to 'mop-up' members or offer 'therapy'. People will be asked to say what they want before others in the group respond; and
- Individuals identify their own support outside the group in case they want or need it.

Throughout the work, we talked about the effect that group membership had on relationships in the agency and more widely, sharing worries, surprises and strategies. The ground-rules for the group were revisited frequently as members checked whether what was happening was what had been agreed. For those of us experienced in group work, ground-rules can become a formal stage in which assumptions have already been made (NISW, 1993) rather than a dynamic, inclusive process. The skills of creating and using them required discussion and clarification, rehearsal, monitoring and review and, after the group had finished, evaluation and consolidation.

At the first meeting of the group, an exercise was used to introduce members to symbolic representation and its potential in accessing experience in different ways (Milner, 1987; Cox and Theilgaard, 1997; Gersie, 1997). The exercise also set the context of a 'public' self, which others see and 'know', and a 'private' self, which is hidden, possibly from choice or lack of language to communicate this. Women were encouraged to start to share some information about their lives and listen to each other without taking on responsibility. This acted as a rehearsal for the subsequent work and reinforced control over what was chosen and how much was shared.

Metaphors chosen and their impact

A wide variety of projects or metaphors were chosen and achieved different degrees of completion. A model of a roller-coaster was finished within the first few sessions of the group. It represented one woman's feelings of being out of control, and then held considerable significance for the way these subsequently changed. After the group finished she wrote to say: 'The group came at the right time for me. My life has completely turned around'. This is consistent with the changes she has made in her life. An embroidery and collage tree remained unfinished, and a set of cross-stitch plaques saying 'It's not my fault' became one member's closing gift for participants. Other projects such as a papier-maché sculpture, and a carrier bag with a tangle of differently coloured wool, remained in the individual's imagination but were no less real for that.

As women worked on their projects their understanding of them and relationship to them changed. For example, the tree was conceived initially with the top and branches being 'good things' and below ground were the negative or 'bad' memories. Difficulties about where to put things that were ambiguous cut through this artificial separation and encouraged a more integrated reflection: 'You can't go back and get just one memory can you? Everything comes with it.' Fragments of memory were seen as important, as if they were bits of different jigsaws, each valuable in themselves. Women found themselves thinking about their lives in new ways, both through their work on the projects and through being listened to in a fashion to which they were largely unaccustomed. Reflecting on the group, one woman said, 'You go to all these meetings and everything else, but the one thing you don't do is talk about yourself. And that's what it encouraged you to do – to talk about yourself. You're usually sat there doing something for everyone else.' The fact of us being all women and all mothers meant that some things seemed easy to talk about as shared experience. However, the differences in engagement and disclosure were indicative of substantial diversity and confirmed the importance of careful and respectful listening rather than pressure to conform.

The principle findings of the research were the individual women's self-discoveries. My analysis of the post-group interviews took place in the context of my experience of the groups and continued contact with the agency.

Additional findings

- The importance of careful contracting in setting up a group which includes the development of transferable skills such as self-responsibility;
- The power of metaphor to 'hold' meaning and protect privacy. Some women used it more easily than others did, but all found it interesting;

- Shared intimacy resulted in a higher degree of trust and respect between group members both during and after the group;
- Individuals had a higher level of confidence in themselves, respecting their own and others' weaknesses as normal, and had more trust in the validity of their own feelings; and
- Individuals welcomed the expectation of self-responsibility. All said it was more difficult to watch and listen to someone in distress than to be that person.

Issues and dilemmas

Participation in the group was affected by a wide variety of complex factors and it is possible that the expectation that women find a metaphor and use the group to explore it is yet another pressure that could lead to feelings of failure. Women participated at different levels; one woman attended only twice and never spoke about a project. However, she was keen to participate in the follow-up interviews and said that she had enjoyed hearing other people's ideas.

Having been worried about their capacity not to reach out to each other or 'mop-up' as one woman called it, this was actually seen as one of the most helpful features of the group. Reflections about this included: 'I think it was hard to let that carry on like that, but it was good in the long run.'; another woman described it as 'emotional licence'. Women experienced discomfort at seeing other members in distress, but the reported experience of being that woman was of remaining in control throughout. This sympathetic curiosity and careful distance is something which is familiar to research interviewers (Martin, 1995; Fook *et al.*, 1999; Birch and Miller, 2000). It was also a position or skill that service users, and professionals, could learn to use in their own lives, both in listening to others and in attending to themselves.

We explored the issue of privacy, because the women had very little space emotionally or physically that was exclusive and private. This meant that work on the projects was mostly in very public space, which the 'private' family is for mothers in particular. Women reported that they developed their ideas without thinking about them consciously, and found ways of deflecting family interest in what they were doing. Strategies included telling family members that projects were something connected with a course, working at times when they were alone, or choosing an activity that they already did, such as sewing. Storage for projects was found under the bed or on the top of a wardrobe, and most women chose not to discuss the meaning of the work with anyone outside the group.

I was also conscious that these women would continue to have contact with each other, often daily, after the group had finished, and felt concern that they might be left exposed by the work. Similarly, their relationships with friends and family were likely to be affected by any changes in the way they thought about who they were and what they wanted. At all stages in the process women were encouraged to think about this and manage it for themselves. The follow-up interviews therefore also included questions about this.

Ethical issues and power relationships

In reflecting on this group as a piece of research with service users I have found myself challenged by a series of definitions that do not do justice to the nature and complexity of the relationships, and the processes involved in this and similar work. First, the definition of this group as 'service users' implies a clarity and cohesion in the group, which is not accurate. While all members of the group had used the services of the project at some time (my own children had been part of the crèche provision when younger), there was also a wide range of relationships to the project and to each other before the group began. Some women were involved in crèche work, voluntary and paid sessional work, and the project co-ordinator was also a member of the group. While the range of roles women occupied and the resulting complexity of power relationships was particularly visible in this project, it is likely that relationships in any group will be diverse and complex (Morris, 1993; NISW, 1993). I have been asked how I negotiated my roles as participant, facilitator and researcher in the group. This question implies that those most affected by potential conflict are the professionals or 'researchers'. In practice, research changes the lives of all those involved. When conducting research with service users, we are required to manage complexities of perspective, role and identity, and to recognise that these are not exclusive to professionals.

In designing any piece of research we should be prepared to construct meaning together, and to share the knowledge and skills we have. Michelle McCarthy's work on the sexuality of women with learning disabilities refers to the difficulties of involving service users in research, especially because of resources and understandings (McCarthy, 1999). With this in mind, I believe that the different research interests and questions of the 'service user' and the 'academic'[3] can and should be made explicit without removing the capacity for involvement, or becoming tokenistic or patronising. In response to the women's original interest, I was open about my research agenda. While I found, like Michelle McCarthy, that their issues and concerns were related directly to their daily lives and relationships, they saw no difficulty in accommodating both agendas. So while it may not always be possible to start from a service-user initiative, it may be less problematic than we think.

Definitions of inclusive research need to include auto-ethnography, oral history and critical autobiography, for example, and to recognise the coexistence of different research methods and agendas, in which the service users' agenda is primary. In considering the merits of different methods, we need to consider fitness for purpose and the degree to which those chosen contribute to the disruption of 'normal' power relationships.

Transferable principles
- Research with service users should strengthen voices that are less heard;
- When service users set the agenda it may be in the form of an expressed interest rather than a research question;
- 'Academics' can offer skills and techniques to support that agenda, and may have a separate agenda of their own; and
- Different agendas are not necessarily mutually exclusive and can be negotiated.

Conclusion
Stories have transformative potential (McAdams, 1993) and creative autobiography is one way of helping people to achieve what Linden West describes as subjective cohesion and agency in their own lives (West, 2000). The work is concerned with strengthening the voices of the silenced rather than interpreting and further silencing. In this respect, 'academics' are there to respond to the 'service users' agenda rather than to impose their own. Peter Beresford describes service user involvement as taking the different forms of 'comment' and 'control' (Beresford, 1993). In this research, participants were able to comment on my agenda while remaining fully in control of their own. Finally, it is important to recognise that the process the women were engaged in was one of research, and not therapy, although the boundaries between these activities are clearly permeable (Birch and Miller, 2000).

Note:
1. I believe that the distinction between staff and users is unclear and unhelpful in an organisation that encourages service users to do paid and unpaid work and to manage the project. The terms are used here to distinguish between salaried staff and others.

2. This refers to the production of one's autobiography for the purpose of illuminating a social issue.

3. As I have already argued, these definitions are not mutually exclusive. I use the terms 'service users' and 'academic' to differentiate between the interests and agendas of those involved without implying that the service users are not researchers.

References

Bender, M and Cheston, R (2000) *Understanding Dementia: The man with the worried eyes* London, Jessica Kingsley

Beresford, P (1993) 'A programme for change: Current issues in user involvement and empowerment' in Beresford, P and Harding, T (eds) *A Challenge to Change: Practical Experiences of Building User-led Services* London, NISW

Birch, M and Miller, T (2000) 'Involving Intimacy: The interview as therapeutic opportunity' *International Journal of Social Research Methodology*, 3 (3) pp 189–202

Bornat, J, Dimmock, B, Jones, D and Peace, S (2000) 'Researching the Implications of Family Change for Older People: The contribution of a life history approach' in Chamberlayne, P, Bornat, J and Wengraf, T (eds) *The Turn to Biographical Methods in Social Science: Comparative issues and examples*, London, Routledge

Butler, A (2000) 'Only for My-self: Creative autobiography as an intimate therapeutic medium' *Auto/Biography* VIII(1&2) pp 49–56

Chamberlayne, P, Bornat, J and Wengraf, T (eds) (2000), *The Turn to Biographical Methods in Social Science: comparative issues and examples* London, Routledge

Cox, M and Theilgaard, A (1997) *Mutative Metaphors in Psychotherapy: The Aeolian mode* London, Tavistock

Fook, J, Munford, R and Sanders, J (1999) 'Interviewing and evaluating' in Shaw, I and Lishman, J (eds) *Evaluation and Social Work Practice* London, Sage

Gersie, A (1997) *Reflections on Therapeutic Storymaking: The use of stories in groups* London, Jessica Kingsley

Greenhalgh, T and Hurwitz, B (1999) 'Why study narrative?' *The British Medical Journal*, 318

Griffiths, M (1995) *Feminisms and the Self: The web of identity* London, Routledge

Laird, J (1994) 'Changing women's narratives: Taking back the discourse' in Davis, L V (ed.) *Building on Women's Strengths: A Social Work Agenda for the 21st Century* New York, Haworth Press

Martin, R (1995) *Oral History in Social Work: Research, assessment and intervention* London, Sage

McAdams, D P (1993) *Stories We Live by: Personal Myths and the Making of the Self* New York, Guilford Press

McCarthy, M (1999) *Sexuality and Women with Learning Difficulties* London, Jessica Kingsley

Mies, M (1983) 'Towards a methodology for feminist research' in Bowles, G and Klein, R D (eds) *Theories of Women's Studies* London, Routledge & Kegan Paul

Milner, M (1987) *Eternity's Sunrise: A way of keeping a diary* London, Virago

Morris, J (1993) 'Working together (1): The expression of choice' in Beresford, P and Harding, T (eds) *A Challenge to Change: Practical experiences of building user-led services* London, NISW

NISW, The User-centred Services Group (1993) *Building Bridges between People Who Use and People Who Provide Services* London, NISW

Saukko, P (1995) 'Anorexia Nervosa: Rereading the stories that became me' *Cultural Studies* (1)

West, L (2001) *Doctors on the Edge: GPs, health and learning in the inner city* London, Free Association Books

White, M and Epston, D (1990) *Narrative Means to Therapeutic Ends* New York, W. W. Norton

CHAPTER 4
Planning and Evaluating Practice: Clients' Contribution
Vered Slonim-Nevo

Evaluating practice: the contribution of the clients

It is well accepted that clinical work should be evaluated systematically. Evaluation is needed to determine effectiveness and the direction of the treatment, involving the client in the treatment process, accountability, providing data about clients and their problems to agency policy decision-makers, and developing empirically based models of practice (Briar and Blythe, 1985; Tripodi, 1994; Bloom *et al.*, 1995). The purpose of this chapter is to demonstrate how enabling clients to be active participants throughout the evaluation process could contribute to both problem solving and evaluation endeavour. One method of evaluation, single-case design, will be focused on in this text:

> *Single-case design is often used to assess the effectiveness of clinical interventions with individuals, families or groups. Unlike traditional approaches, in which external researchers using experimental and quasi-experimental group designs evaluate the work of clinicians, single-case methodology enables clinicians and their clients to evaluate their shared counselling work. The method requires an explicit definition of the problem or treatment goal, a clear definition of the intervention strategy, and repeated measures of the problem before and during the treatment process. The results are recorded in graph form to denote the extent of progress over time. The single-case design recording process enables clinicians and clients to compare both visually and statistically, the extent of achieved progress during the intervention phases against baseline information. This knowledge enables to draw conclusions about the success of the treatment, the continuation of an intervention showing positive results, the option of selecting another intervention strategy, or the need to terminate an ineffective procedure.* (Gingerich, 1983; Bloom *et al.*, 1995)

The methodology of single-case design is user-friendly to both clinicians and clients (Slonim-Nevo and Ziv, 1998). Moreover, recent results suggest that evaluation via single-case design affects the treatment's outcomes (Slonim-Nevo and Anson, 1988). Specifically, among a study population of juvenile delinquents who were treated by probation officers, it was found that the experimental group participants – those whose treatment was

45

evaluated by single-case design – reduced the frequency of their arrests by police significantly, whereas their control group counterparts' rate increased.

There are several possible explanations for these promising results (Slonim-Nevo and Anson, 1998). In this chapter, we emphasise one of them: clients are empowered and thus improve because they are regarded as significant participants in their own treatment. Below I shall look at the opportunity to engage clients in the various stages of the evaluation process via the methodology of single-case design. The process of evaluation will be described and the scope for engaging clients at each stage will be illustrated.

Stage 1: Specifying problems/goals
Definition
Single-case design evaluation requires that one or more of the client's problems or goals be selected and defined operationally (Slonim-Nevo, 1997). This procedure is inherent in many of the existing therapeutic models that are directed at solving or improving the client's presenting problem (for example, behavioural therapy, cognitive intervention, family therapy, and brief counselling (Berg, 1994; Cooper, 1990; Rabin, 1981, Slonim-Nevo and Vosler, 1991).

Client's participation
Single-case design evaluation provides an opportunity to share the process of selecting and defining a goal for treatment between the clinician and the client, an activity that can be re-initiated at any time during the treatment process. The key element to be addressed when clinicians and clients select jointly a goal for treatment is the client's priorities and wishes. This is based on the assumption that, focusing on the client's priorities rather than on diagnosis, is more likely to yield successful results (Berg, 1994). Since the emphasis is on a joint dialogue, clinicians should add their professional experience as well. The following example is taken from a conversation by the author with a single mother who sought help for her adolescent boy who was refusing to attend school because of severe anxiety attacks. These attacks had been treated previously by various agencies, including outpatient treatment, emergency shelter, and psychiatric hospitalisation. The first part of the conversation is aimed at selecting the problem for treatment, while the second focuses on defining the problem.

> *Mother*: I don't know where to start. Ben did not go to school at all this year. He says that he is afraid of the children at school. He stays up all night and sleeps during the day. But the worst thing is how he fights with his brother Gil. He is so jealous of him that he screams at him the

moment he comes home from school. I try to separate them, but he yells at me too and even pushes me, so I take Gil and we go to the streets until late at night to avoid Ben. I myself am not healthy, I had breast cancer a few years ago and I do not have the time to go for a check-up.

Clinician: There are so many problems that you deal with every day. I value your ability to carry on and to try again to make it better even after so many trials that I understand were not very helpful.

Mother: I have no choice. I go on because of the children. If something happens to me no one will take care of them. But sometimes I think that I cannot take it any more, particularly when Ben screams so loud that I am afraid that the neighbours will call the police.

Clinician: I am here to help. Let me see if I understand correctly. You actually wish to change three difficulties in your life: Ben not going to school, the fights at home, and your physical weakness. Am I right?

Mother: Almost. I don't worry about my health, whatever happens to me is not that important. But I also worry about Gil who is failing at school and has to be in the streets because of his brother.

Clinician: I see, so we add a fourth issue: Gil's learning. But I think that even though you don't worry about your health, I do and I wish to have this issue in our list.

Mother: Okay.

Clinician: So the list now has Ben's school, Gil's grades, the fights at home, and your health. Where would you like to start?

Mother: It is hard to decide because one problem is connected with the others. You see if Ben was at school with friends, he'd be less lonely and then he wouldn't abuse his brother.

Clinician: So do you want us to start with Ben going to school?

Mother: Well, as much as this is important to me I think I'd like first to reduce the violence at home. It is summer now anyway, so we can worry about school later.

Clinician: It makes a lot of sense. What about your health? Could you at least meet with your doctor so that we'll know that you are okay? It is hard for me to focus on your sons while worrying that you are neglecting your health.

Mother: Okay, I will go with a friend because I am afraid to go on my own.

Clinician: That's great. So let's focus on Ben's behaviour. Let's try to define the problem so that we'll be able to follow it and see if it gets better. Can you describe specifically what is going on when Ben is abusive, and you and Gil are fleeing your home?

Mother: The moment he sees Gil entering our home from school he starts provoking him, insulting him, and even pushing him physically. I try to interfere, but he yells at me and he might push me if I try to stop his attacks.

Clinician: So we can define the problem as screaming, insulting, pushing and physically attacking you and Gil?

Mother: Yes, that's right.

Clinician: So, if we decide right now that 1 is the worst condition in terms of Ben's behaviour and 9 is the best, where would you place him today?

Mother: On 1, it has been terrible at home lately.

Clinician: How would you like it to be? We know what 1 looks like, how does 9 feel?

Mother: It feels great. I come home from work, Ben is relaxed. Gil comes home and does his homework, I make dinner, we eat together, we talk, and we watch TV. It is quiet.

Clinician: That does sound like a nice evening. So you evaluate the problem to be on 1 now. Where would you like it to be in three months from now so that counselling will be worthwhile?

Mother: On 9, of course.

Clinician: I am afraid you over estimate my skills. Let's try to be more modest.

Mother: Okay, 8 or 7.

Clinician: I like to suggest the number 6, because it really is a big move from 1 to 6, and 6 is more than half way through.

Mother: Okay, 6 will be better than what we have now. I think this conversation made things clearer to me.

Stage 2: Selecting the Design
Definition:
The next stage is the selection of an evaluation design. It is possible to work with sophisticated designs that improve the ability to determine whether the intervention itself, and not other external factors (for example, maturation or

instrumentation), explain the change in the client's condition. It is also possible to select simple designs that are less capable of showing a direct link between treatment and change, but are user-friendly and fit well with clinical settings.

Client's participation
Ordinarily, it is the clinicians who select the design, based on the amount of time and energy they wish to devote to the evaluation process, while clients usually do not take part in this endeavour. Apparently, in the literature on single-case design, there is not a single example in which clients participate in the selection of the evaluation design, nor is it recommended to do so.

Yet, planning the evaluation process together could be beneficial to both clinicians and their clients. Clients who are consulted about the design to be selected may become ambitious and encourage the selection of more complex designs. Having shared the decision of which design to use, clients will be more likely to cooperate with data collection as well as with delays or obstacles, such as reversing to baseline or initiating the process with a baseline phase. Moreover, clients are likely to enjoy gaining knowledge about research, being regarded as intelligent partners, and contemplating the notion that therapy can be viewed as a mutual detective journey.

Stage 3: Measuring the problem or the goal for treatment
Definition
A key element in the methodology of single-case design is repeated measures of the client's problem before and during the treatment process. While standardised scales may be used, self-made scales specifically devised to assess the client's unique condition are often utilised. Self-made scales are either self-anchored or rating scales. The self-anchored scales are built jointly by the clinicians and the clients to measure the clients' feelings, thoughts, and actions. The clients describe the worst scenario and the best scenario, and the descriptions are placed on a scale (for example, 1 is the worst and 7 is the best). Rating scales are similar, but someone else (a teacher or a parent) defines the points on the scale and records the data (Bloom *et al.*, 1995).

Client's participation
Traditionally, when clinicians/evaluators ask clients to fill out standardised scales, they regard the clients as respondents and not as partners. Even when clinicians and clients jointly construct self-made scales, the role of the clients is to provide the necessary information and not to share the decision about the type of measures to be utilised. Thus, if clients are partners and not just respondents, they will need to learn about various types of measures and their

different qualities. Clinicians will not become teachers of research methods, but they will provide a few straightforward explanations on measurement.

Beyond an ideological wish to view clients as partners and to share with them knowledge and power, this mutual consultation about measurement is also likely to promote data collection. That is, clients will be more likely to fill out forms at home, less likely to provide biased data, and more likely to spend time and energy on measurement. Moreover, when clients are engaged in the selection of measures, they will be likely to understand the results obtained, and thus have the ability to draw conclusions about the effectiveness of the intervention. The following conversation illustrates how this joint activity could be performed with a relatively short explanation:

Clinician: I think it is important to assess carefully how angry you feel towards your husband right now and perhaps in the future, so that we will be able to see whether our meetings improve the relationship.

Client: Okay.

Clinician: There are several ways to measure a problem, and each has advantages and disadvantages. Would you like to know about that?

Client: Yes, why not?

Clinician: When trying to assess the quality of marital relations, we can use ready-made scales that are called standardised scales, and we use them in research. We have, for example, a scale with 25 items that takes about five minutes to fill out and we get a score between 0 and 100, with higher numbers indicating more problems. The advantage of this scale is that it was tested in other studies and we know that a score above 30 means real marital problems. But there are other options as well. Together we can build a very simple scale from 1 to 9, in which 1 means the worst situation between you and your husband and 9 the best. We can describe those two points and than you can amend it from time to time. This is a self-made scale that we can build together to fit your own situation. We can also record simple things that are important to you, such as the number of times each day that you talk, go out, etc., and see over time if there is any improvement. What do you think you like the most?

Client: I think I like the idea of looking at real things like going out and talking. We went to many therapists in the past and talking was not very helpful.

Clinician: Okay, we call it self-observation of behaviour. You know, recording this may affects the relationships as it is with people who record how many cigarettes they smoke each day.

Client: So it may actually help?.

Clinician: Yes, but in terms of getting objective results it is a problem. It is called reactivity, a measure that changes the results just by using it.

Client: Never mind, I would like to look at real changes in the relationship.

Clinician: Okay, what do you suggest you should look at? And how often – every day, every week? We also need to think how would you record this at home.

Client: I think what you said earlier, how many times a week we go out and how many times a day we talk. Maybe we can also look at how many times in a week we fight.

Clinician: So you will record perhaps every night before you go to sleep how many fights you had that day, and how many times you talked?

Client: Yes, and every Saturday night how many times we went out.

Clinician: Good!

Stage 4: Selecting the intervention
Definition
Intervention in single-case design is analogous to the independent variable in experimental research designs. Therefore, it is important to state clearly what the treatment is, and describe it in concrete terms (Rosen, 1993). Clinicians may find it difficult, or even undesirable, to define in advance the specific details of the treatment. However, they can describe in general terms what intervention they wish to employ. After the initial evaluation of the situation, clinicians are likely to have some ideas about how to help their clients. They may have a plan about whom to invite to the meetings; they are likely to have some ideas about what to do first; and they generally know what type of therapeutic orientation they tend to use, and with what techniques they feel comfortable. This general description is important in single-case design, because it provides an idea about the treatment to be evaluated, even though all may change during the therapeutic process and a new description be needed (Slonim-Nevo, 1997).

Clients' participations
Generally, clinicians tend not to share the decision about the type of treatment to be used with their clients. Perhaps this is based on an assumption that clients like to have skillful therapists who know what to do, and having the therapist consult them may be perceived as there being a lack of professional authority. Some clients may, in fact, prefer a clinician who takes

charge straight away and does not confuse them with too many alternatives, but others may appreciate learning about various therapeutic options and share the decision about the therapeutic method to be tried.

Clinicians may share with clients what they think may be helpful, details of their professional skills, and what are the advantages and disadvantages of each option. Clients may share with clinicians their past experiences with therapy, what was helpful and what was not, their likes and dislikes, and their perceptions about what kind of intervention might help. Clients and clinicians may then weigh up each option and together reach a decision. Clinicians, from time to time, particularly when asked specifically by the clients about various therapeutic options, do discuss this matter with their clients. But this is not done regularly, and when it is discussed, it is more in the manner of providing information rather than making a joint decision on the type of intervention to be selected.

Clients who share this decision are more likely to share responsibility for the success of the process as well. Moreover, they may enjoy gaining new information, being treated as equals and not just as 'patients', and realising that their own experience and knowledge is important. Clinicians, who regard their clients as partners may give up some of their professional power, and perhaps some of their therapeutic manoeuvres, but they are likely to be more effective because they will be able to use the experiences of their clients. The following conversation is a transcript of a conversation between the author and a woman suffering from depression, starting with the segment in which various options are discussed:

Client: So you see I have been in therapy for years and with not much help.

Clinician: You know precisely because you saw so many therapists and tried so many methods already, it is important that we decide together where to start, and that we learn form your experiences in the past.

*Clien*t: I don't know, I take medications and it does help a little, and I tried for years to understand why, and we talked about my mother and my childhood, and I see how it is related, but still I am so unhappy and worried and cry all the time.

Clinician: So we can say that medications help, but going over your childhood again and again is not helpful.

Client: Yes.

Clinician: You know, I'd like to share with you some of the methods that I have tried in the past and they may help you as well. I am not sure, but let's try to think together where to start. We can also decide to combine a few methods together.

Client: Um...

Clinician: One time with a woman who was in great pain, a strict regime of exercise got her out of the initial depression and then we were able to do other things. Actually, there is research evidence showing that serious exercising can improve mood.

Client: Um...

Clinician: Also, you know, sometimes I invite other family members, and especially the wife or the husband, to the meetings. Often, without even knowing it, family members behave in ways that increases the depression. So this is also an option we may consider. Have you tried this in the past? What do you think?

Client: To be honest, exercise is not for me. But I don't mind bringing my husband. What will you tell him? But I don't like to involve my daughters; they have their own worries.

Clinician: What we will try to do together is to observe very carefully how he reacts to your moods, because you live together so he might have an impact. Then, we can see which of his behaviours make it better for you, and which make it worse.

Client: I am not sure there is a connection, but we can try.

Clinician: Yes, and we will measure how you feel every week so that if you continue to f*eel down, we can try something else.*

Stage 5: Analysing the data and drawing conclusions
Definition
In single-case design, the results are placed on a graph. On the horizontal axes we denote the time (meetings, weeks, months), and on the vertical axes the values of the scale that measures the problem (e.g., 1–9, 0–100, etc.). Each phase in the design is marked with a capital letter (A, B, etc.); a vertical line separates between each phase; and the various data points are connected with a line. At any time during the therapeutic process, both the clinician and the client may observe the results and draw tentative or more definite conclusions. (*Bloom et al.*, 1995)

There are two basic methods of analysing the data: visual analysis and statistical analysis (Gingerich, 1983). In visual analysis, we observe the magnitude of change in the client's condition during the intervention phases versus the baseline phases, the stability of the change, and how soon it occurred. There are specific guidelines for such analysis, but even untrained observers are able to detect positive, negative or no change over time. Statistical analysis requires more training, and therefore cannot easily be shared between clinician and client. Based on the results, it is possible to determine whether a specific intervention should be continued, which intervention among alternatives is the most effective, and whether or not the client is getting better.

Clients' participation

Clinician and client may observe the results jointly at any point in time during the process in order to make a joint decision about the therapy and to draw tentative and final conclusions. The ability to observe the results on a graph enhances the possibility of obtaining a clear understanding of the situation. The example below is taken from the experience of a social worker working in the rehabilitation unit of the Social Security Office in Israel (Slonim-Nevo and Ziv, 1998). This example illustrates how observations were used to stimulate joint insight into the client's behaviour patterns.

A widow with young children sought help because of depressed moods and concerns about her inability to keep her house clean. Three measures were used to assess her condition: a standardised scale measuring satisfaction with life, a self-made scale assessing her daily mood, and an anchored scale recording her level of satisfaction with the physical condition of the house. Figure 4.1 illustrates one segment of the intervention phase (B), suggesting an apparent connection between the client's mood and her perception of the physical condition of the house. In four out of the seven points of data collection, when the mood perception was high, the client thought that her house was neglected. When she was satisfied with the physical condition of the house her mood perception was lower.

When the client observed the graph she said: 'I think this is because when I don't worry about cleaning I take the children out and we are having a good time and I feel better, but when I clean the house, I pay no attention to the children and then I hate myself for neglecting them' (Slonim-Nevo and Ziv, 1998, p. 437). Based on these results, the client was able to lower her expectations about tidiness and concentrate on her and her children's emotional needs.

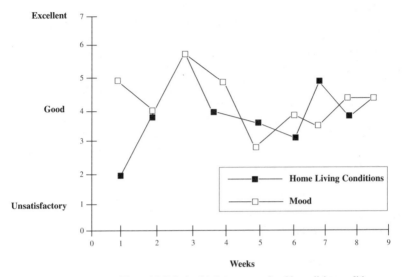

Figure 4.1: Relationship between mood and home living conditions
Source: Slonim-Nevo and Ziv (1978), p. 435.

Concluding remarks

The methodology of single-case design, used to evaluate the effectiveness of clinical interventions, provides a unique opportunity to regard clients as partners throughout the evaluation/counselling process. Such a perspective may contribute both to the clients' conditions and to the evaluation procedure. During the first stage of the journey, clinician and client together select the goal for the therapy, and define it in concrete terms. This activity usually helps to clarify the client's situation and to focus on concrete and achievable treatment goals. Then, the clinician and the client select jointly an evaluation design, the measures to be used, and decide together the preferred methods of intervention. These activities are normally rarely shared with clients. Yet it is possible to perform them jointly if there is a will to take the extra time and effort and provide clients with basic information on measurement, and treatment alternatives. Such co-operation, it is claimed, is not only likely to increase clients' willingness to collect data and tolerate the evaluation's requirements, but it is also likely to have a positive affect on their condition. Moreover, clients are likely to enjoy being regarded as partners, are likely to appreciate gaining new knowledge, may enjoy the adventure elements of the evaluation process, and are likely to appreciate the clinicians' willingness to invest time and energy on their behalf.

References

Berg, I K (1994) *Family Based Services: A solution-focused approach* New York, W. W. Norton

Bloom, M, Fischer, J, and Orme, J G (1995) *Evaluating Practice: Guidelines for the accountable professional* Boston, MA, Allyn and Bacon

Briar, S and Blythe, B J (1985) 'Agency support for evaluating the outcomes of social work services' *Administration in Social Work*, 9(2), pp 25–36

Cooper, M (1990) 'Treatment of a client with obsessive-compulsive disorder' *Social Work Research and Abstracts* (June), pp 26–32

Gingerich, W J (1983) 'Significant testing in single-subject research' in Rosenblatt, A and Waldfogel,D (eds) *Handbook of Clinical Social Work* San Francisco, CA, Jossey-Bass, pp 694–720

Hudson, W W (1982) *The Clinical Measurement Package: A field manual* Homewood, IL, Dorsey Press

Rabin, C (1981) 'The single-case design in family therapy evaluation research' *Family Process*, 20, pp 351–63

Rosen, A (1993) 'Systemic planned practice' *Social Service Review*, (March), pp 84–100

Slonim-Nevo, V (1997) 'Evaluating social work practice: The dual roles of the clinician and the evaluator' *Families in Society*, 78, pp 228–39

Slonim-Nevo, V and Anson, J (1998) 'Evaluating Practice: Does it improve treatment?' *Social Work Research*, 22(2), pp 66–74

Slonim-Nevo,V and Vosler, N R (1991) 'The use of single-system design with systemic brief problem-solving therapy' *Families in Society*, 72(1), pp 38–44

Slonim-Nevo, V and Ziz, E (1998) 'Training social workers to evaluate practice: perceptions after one and three years' *International Social Work*, 41 (4), pp 431–42

Tripodi, T (1994) *A Primer on Single Subject Design for Clinical Social Workers* Washington, DC, NASW Press

CHAPTER 5
An Action Evaluation as a Tool to Engage Users and Practitioners
Barbara Fawcett

There are many ways of carrying out evaluations. This is an account of an evaluation which evolved, developed and changed over time. The project to be evaluated was a European Union (EU) funded initiative to enable people from local Asian communities who had experienced mental health problems, re-enter the workforce. It was agreed clearly at the outset that it would be an 'action evaluation'. Accordingly, the evaluation was designed to be inclusive and participative, with findings feeding continually into and informing policy, practice and service developments.

The money for the two-year project followed a successful bid by a service-user orientated mental health organisation located in the voluntary sector. This organisation served a large northern city in the United Kingdom with sizeable Asian communities.[1] The voluntary organisation had found itself catering to a largely white male grouping and, by means of another locally-funded project developed in association with the local social services department, had succeeded in increasing the numbers of Asian women using the organisation by introducing 'women only' days, and textile design and batik-card-making workshops. Women-only therapeutic groups also proved popular with Asian women, although it remained difficult to attract and retain those with longer-term and enduring mental health problems. This initial venture had set out not only to increase the number of Asian women using the scheme, but also to increase the number of Asian women employed by the scheme. The introduction of an active volunteer programme had enabled those without qualifications to enrol on NVQ (National Vocational Qualifications) courses, and to obtain paid employment in the statutory sector and in the voluntary and private sectors.

The 'action evaluation' set out to be a participative exercise. However, as has been highlighted frequently in the field of mental health and in other areas, participation means different things to different groups of people, and it is important to clarify from the outset what is meant and how this will operate in the designated context (see, for example, Beresford and Trevillion, 1995; Fawcett, 2000). An important starting point relates to service user perspectives on research. User movements in the field of disability, and organisations such as the Nuffield Foundation (1996) have pointed out that service users do not want to be treated as objects of investigation. They stress that all research should have an agreed and documented value base, with the levels of 'participation' being clearly defined. They also emphasise that research needs to be justified in terms of service-user priorities, and that the case for carrying out research needs to be made clearly to ensure that the money made available would not be better spent on improving a service. Faulkner and Layzell (2000) have emphasised, in a report produced for the Mental Health Foundation, that the process of being involved in a research project can increase self-confidence and can be a liberating experience. They also point out that user-led research projects, not surprisingly, focus on those areas viewed as being important by service users. These areas include the development and operation of a holistic approach to care and support; a focus on supportive networks; full service-user choice relating to responses, including alternative and complementary therapies; open access drop-in and self-help groups; sensitivity to religious practices and beliefs; and the involvement of independent user groups in service policy, planning and delivery.

This project discussed in this chapter was not a user-led research project in the sense that it was not initiated by service users. The funding for the project had been applied for by the voluntary organisation, and while those involved in the bid included representatives from Asian community groupings and other voluntary organisations working in the field of mental health, those involved at this stage thought that it could be counter-productive to involve service users in case the bid was unsuccessful. The proposed project also involved moving the voluntary organisation into a new area, and as such there was not an existing group of service users to draw upon. This highlights a dilemma about involvement. Service users engaged in other aspects of the voluntary organisation, provided that they agreed to spend the necessary time and energy and develop with the existing staff group necessary support mechanisms, could have been fully engaged in the bid from the outset. However, this particular project set out to be developmental. The brief was to maximise service-user involvement, and as the project was a new venture it was envisaged that involvement and participation would be incremental. Accordingly, from the outset, all those involved in setting up the project and obtaining the funding, including representatives from Asian community groups and the local voluntary and statutory services, became members of the project management board. The formative 'action evaluation' of the project was designated a major agenda item at project management board meetings and it was agreed that the process of evaluation and the information generated would be reviewed regularly and used to inform the development of the project. It was also agreed that the workers appointed to the project would sit on the management board and that, as the project developed, service-user representatives would become board members with their training and advocacy needs being addressed, and their expenses, child care and transport needs being met. Consideration was also given to remunerating the service users financially, and while all were in favour of doing this, in practice, financial constraints rendered it a difficult option to pursue. It was also envisaged that the project workers would hold their own weekly meetings, and that, again, the evaluation would become a regular and major item for consideration.

The 'action evaluation' framework adopted is described in Box 1 below. This framework draws on many different evaluative approaches (for example, Cheetham *et al.*, 1992; Hart and Bond, 1995; Pawson and Tilley, 1997; Evans and Fisher, 1999) and is designed to be both flexible and easy to use.

Box 1: An action evaluation framework

Involve	All those connected with the project (for example, service users, project workers, managers).
Clarify	The level of involvement.
Produce	An ethical statement for all participants.
Outline	The current situation (baseline information).
Specify	The available resources;
	The overall aim and the specific objectives of the project;
	The long-term outcomes and time-scale;
	The medium-term outcomes and time-scale; and
	The short-term outcomes and time-scale.
Link	Each long-term, medium-term and short-term outcome to each specific objective.
Detail	The rationale – why the agreed objectives and outcomes were decided upon and who participated in this process.
Monitor	The activity (impact information).
Review	The progress (or lack of it) towards the specified long-term, medium-term and short-term outcomes.
Detail	Why progress (or the lack of it) has occurred.
Review	The objectives and specified outcomes.
Document	The changes to the objectives and specified outcomes.
Feed	The findings into the development of the project.
	repeat
Complete	The evaluation by writing a report highlighting the key points from the previous documentation.

As discussed, as part of the evaluative process, the level of involvement of project management board members, project workers and service users was clarified at the outset, and this area was revisited as the project progressed. The project management board decided initially that an Asian woman with extensive experience of working in the voluntary mental health sector would be employed to collect the evaluative information, and to monitor activity. This would enable regular progress reports to be presented to the representative project management group and to the project workers group and would enable the project to be appraised continually and further developed in line with the findings.

At the outset, an ethical statement was produced to apply to project management board members, project workers and service users, and all those involved in the evaluation. This statement gave details of the project and the 'action evaluation', and highlighted how the information produced by the evaluation would influence the project. Confidentiality was assured for all service users, and the statement also recognised the operational position of those employed by the project and emphasised that the changes agreed would focus on the identified needs of the project rather than on the working practices of individual project workers.

As highlighted, the evaluative framework was designed to be inclusive and straightforward. As a means of introducing the framework to workers and service users, and involving them in the evaluative process, there was an initial emphasis on the collection of baseline information and impact information. Baseline information referred to the situation at the start of the project, and included the numbers of Asian women and men using existing mental health rehabilitative services, their views on these services, and the ways in which these services were linked into rehabilitative and employment opportunities. Other projects were also visited to find out what was working and not working in different contexts, and how those aspects that were found to be working well could be applied successfully to the current project. Additionally, wherever possible, the views of those with mental health problems not using existing rehabilitative services were sought, and their reasons and self-defined needs were discussed.

This interaction served both to publicise the project and to start to engage potential service users and professionals working in the field. It also resulted in those involved in the project, by means of the increasingly representative project management board, reformulating the stated aim of the project. Accordingly, the original aim:

> To enable women and men from local Asian communities, who have experienced mental health problems to enter and re-enter the workforce

> became:

To develop new initiatives and improve existing rehabilitation and employment services to enable improved access to the labour market for women
and men with mental health problems from local Asian communities.

The aim was reformulated in line with the baseline information to reflect
the ways in which employment opportunities for women and men with
mental health problems from Asian communities are affected by a variety of
interacting factors. These include external factors such as employer
prejudice, the disincentives of the benefit system, and a competitive job
market. Aspects such as lack of appropriate guidance and support can also be
highlighted, together with the personal difficulties associated with lack of
confidence, self-esteem and motivation. The project management board, in
the light of the information collected at the start of the project, believed that
there ought to be a greater rehabilitative focus, and one that concentrated on
meeting the self-identified personal developmental needs of project users.

As a result of the evaluative framework, it was also agreed that the project
objectives would be formulated to be as specific as possible. Those writing
about evaluative research (for example, Fulbright-Anderson *et al.*, 1998;
Shaw and Lishman, 1999) continually restate the difficulties faced when
those initiating projects continue to couch objectives in vague and
ambiguous terms. It can also be useful (for example, Pawson and Tilley,
1997) to link objectives to outcomes and additionally to link each objective
to each long-term, medium-term and short-term outcome with the time-scale
for the achievement of each outcome being specified clearly. An example of
this in relation to this project is given in Box 2.

**Box 2: Objectives linked to long-term, medium-term and short-term
outcomes and time-scales for completion**

OBJECTIVE: To produce outreach materials – information and
publicity materials (tapes, local radio, leaflets, telephone helpline) – in
Asian languages to provide information about mental health and mental
health services and the project.

Long-term outcomes:
- The production of accessible leaflets in a variety of languages;
- The production of audio cassettes in a variety of languages; and
- The completion of a series of local radio programmes with Asian
  stations.

Timescale: Two years ▶

◀

Medium-term outcomes:

- The formulation and writing of accessible leaflets in a variety of languages;
- The formulation and taping of the audio cassettes; and
- Negotiation with local radio stations and the writing of a script for a programme on mental health issues.

Timescale: One year

Short-term outcomes:

- Obtaining information on the leaflets/materials available; and
- Canvassing opinion about the information required.

Timescale: Six months

OBJECTIVE: To develop work adjustment/job club activities/co-operative employment opportunities.

Long-term outcomes:

- The operation of a series of work adjustment/job clubs (in different localities, with separate clubs for men and women);
- The establishment of viable co-operative employment opportunities; and
- The establishment of a strategy for tackling external barriers to employment.

Timescale: Two years

Medium-term outcomes:

- The operation of the work adjustment/job clubs maintaining a balance between individual guidance, group training, work adjustment and work placements
- The development with service users of a co-operative catering project and the further development of a textile workshop; and
- The drawing up of a strategy about how external barriers to employment could be tackled.

Timescale: One Year

Short-term outcomes:

- The identification of the barriers to employment experienced by women and men with mental health problems from Asian communities ;
- The exploration of the ways in which these barriers could be addressed by the job clubs; and

▶

◀

- The exploration, with those who feel that they require a longer-term, staged and progressive move into employment and specialist employment, of the range of opportunities which would be attractive and achievable.

Timescale: Six months

OBJECTIVE: To further develop service user participation in the initiative.

Long-term outcome:
- Service users' representatives on the management board supported by service-user forums.

Timescale: Two years

Medium-term outcome:
- Measures to be in place to encourage and support service users to become members of the project management board.

Timescale: One year

Short-term outcomes:
- The identification of existing service user groupings and networks; and
- The exploration of how other initiatives have increased participation.

Timescale: Six months

OBJECTIVE: To further develop effective links with agencies/organisa-tions/groups working in the field of mental health.

Long-term outcomes:
- The development and maintenance of effective links with other agencies/organisations/groups; and
- The presentation of information about project developments to other agencies/organisations/groups.

Timescale: Two years

Medium-term outcomes:
- The development of effective links with other agencies/organisations/groups; and
- The presentation of information about project development to other agencies/organisations/groups.

Timescale: One year ▶

◀

Short-term outcome:

- The mapping of existing provision for Asian women and men who have experienced mental health problems.

Timescale: Six Months

OBJECTIVE: To review and further develop culturally appropriate and ethnically sensitive training for those working in the field of mental health.

Long-term outcomes:

- The production of a training pack for volunteers and staff working in the field of mental health; and
- The operation of training courses for volunteers and staff working in the field of mental health.

Timescale: Two years

Medium-term outcomes:

- Carrying out of the training programme; and
- Compilation of the training pack.

Timescale Eighteen months

Short-term outcomes:

- The review of existing training materials to inform the composition of the training sessions and the compilation of the training pack.

Timescale: Nine months

Explorative formative projects may not find the specific linking of objectives to long-term, medium-term and short-term outcomes appropriate, but short-term and medium-term outcomes framed in this way can serve as performance indicators or project milestones, and ensure that the initiative continues to focus on the agreed objectives and outcomes. Additionally, operating in this way can, if the original objectives and outcomes turn out to be unrealistic given the resources, ensure that change and the reasons for it are well documented. This is important for funding agency monitoring purposes, and to justify and strengthen arguments for additional or longer-term funding. Alternatively, it can be helpful to define the long-term outcome as that which those involved in a project want to have achieved at the end of an agreed time period; the medium-term outcome as relating to process issues; and the short-term outcome as the collection of baseline information, that is the information required at the start of the evaluation in order to move on to the process/action stage.

Although this 'action evaluation' framework is outcome-orientated, process issues are also emphasised by means of a focus on the rationale for the project. This incorporates a review of why the agreed objectives and outcomes were decided upon, and who participated in this process and to what extent. In this context, Pawson and Tilley (1997) and Fullbright-Anderson *et al.*, (1998) have focused on the importance of articulating theories of change, that is exploring why change or movement towards the agreed outcomes either takes place or is absent, as well as examining the underlying factors. An important aspect of this process relates to looking at whether change mechanisms or drivers for change can be transferred to different contexts. An example in relation to the project refers to the specified objective of further developing employment opportunities. Information obtained from Asian women who used existing rehabilitation services at the baseline stage clearly indicated that, for many Asian women, the usual routes to employment were inappropriate. Cultural and family pressures, together with the mental health difficulties they were experiencing, made the goal of external employment unrealistic. However, a reformulated goal directed towards specialist training opportunities and co-operative, women-only forms of employment appeared to be more achievable. The short-term outcome therefore focused on examining, with those who felt that they need a longer-term staged and more pro-gressive route into employment or specialist employment, the range of opportunities which would be attractive and achievable. The medium-term outcome identified specific areas to be developed. These related to a catering enterprise, and the further development of the textile workshop and the volunteer training programme. The longer-term outcome emphasised the sustainable devel-opment of these areas. Discussion with other projects highlighted similar concerns expressed by Asian women, and considerable interest was shown in the development of the specialist areas, the involvement of the women in the develop-ment of these co-operative ventures and the success of the initiatives over time.

Impact information
The next stage in the evaluative framework is to monitor activity or impact. With regard to the project, quantitative information was collected about the number of women and men from local Asian communities using the project, and their key characteristics. This information served additionally to facili-tate the marketing of the project. Qualitative information was also collected. This related to the experiences of those using the project.

A key means of assessing impact is to review the progress (or the lack of it) made towards the specified long-term, medium-term and short-term outcomes within the agreed time-scales. Those aspects that are working well and those that are not in particular situations, can then be highlighted. This process forms a feedback loop. In relation to the project, by means of the feedback loop, progress (or the lack of it) towards the designated outcomes was documented. If, as a result of the information obtained, a decision was made to change an objective and the associated outcomes, then again this was clearly specified. Throughout, the findings were used continually to shape the development of the project. An example here is that one service user expressed the view that the group she had joined was too well established and as a result she felt isolated within the group and unable to participate. Impact information collected showed that because of demand by group participants, some groups had extended the agreed term of the group, and some group participants had rejoined a start-up group. As a result of the concerns expressed, these practices were reviewed by project workers, service users and the project management board, and changes made.

As part of the qualitative monitoring process, in addition to the contribution made by service-user representatives on the project management board, the views of service users and potential service users were obtained for each of the areas referred to specifically by the objectives. In relation to the production of outreach materials, the tapes in Asian languages proved popular, but it was difficult to gauge the utility and effectiveness of the radio programmes. It had been agreed that the numbers of those contacting the telephone contact points given out on air would be collected. However, the range and diversity of the people involved in this information collection exercise rendered this unworkable. Nevertheless, one area to emerge concerned the specified need for a range of language support and interpreting services. These were developed with project workers providing guidance at access points to both project and rehabilitation services, and providing support workers with an informed interpreting service.

In relation to the work adjustment/job clubs, 92 service users were referred or self-referred, to the employment team (See Table 5.1).

Table 5.1 Details about the user population

No of users	Action Plans	Gender	Length of unemployment (%)		Qualifications	Language and literacy problems (%)
92	68	F = 39 M = 29	>1 1yr+ Never worked	4 71 5	No qualification F = 56 M = 41	F = 48 M = 21

All participants worked with the project employment worker to draw up an individualised package or action plan selected from the menu on offer. The menu included individual guidance and reviews, access to training within the programme, support in accessing individual training opportunities, work adjustment workshops, confidence building/assertiveness sessions, support groups, and work placements.

Overall, all those who participated reported that they found the project useful. Information about mental health and knowledge of other services were cited as major benefits, and the majority of participants prioritised these areas rather than work placements and supportive employment elements. Participants highlighted that the project had led to improved communication, language and literacy skills, increased awareness of mental health issues, an increase in self-esteem, and a stronger belief than previously that it was possible to take up training or employment opportunities. Participants also praised the project for being focused on the service user, and for being relaxed, friendly and accepting. Particular strengths identified were that it provided support workers from similar backgrounds and cultures who could speak a variety of Asian languages. The project was also praised for recognising the additional needs of participants.

Table 5.2: Individualised outcomes

	Men	Women
Paid employment	7	5
Working within the project	0	12
Further education	4	7
Work experience	3	6
Voluntary work	4	5
Total	18	35

Several gender differences emerged, in that the majority of the women felt that all aspects of the project would be useful for them, while a small proportion of the men rejected all but the specific work-related elements. Mr G, for example, was referred to the project after being discharged from hospital. He had been diagnosed as suffering from depression. Mr G made it clear from the outset that he was not prepared to discuss emotional, or indeed family, matters, and that his sole reason for attending the project was to find a job. Mr G was aware that some of the men on the project did find it helpful to access other areas, but Mr G refused to acknowledge either his stay in hospital or the possibility that he may have needs additional to that of finding employment. Mr G's wishes were respected by the project, although he was kept informed about all the supportive activities on offer.

As highlighted, the meeting of self-identified personal needs proved to be an important aspect of the project for the majority of the women. Mrs A, for example, a 50-year-old Asian woman who arrived in Britain at the age of eighteen, newly married and not speaking any English, said that she had felt that isolation, low spirits and flagging energy levels had to be accepted as part of daily life. The stigma of appearing not to be coping was so great that she had felt unable to discuss her feelings with her husband's family. Mrs A joined a support group and gradually found that she wanted to talk about her feelings. She also found that she wanted to identify personal areas, such as the development of self-confidence, which she wanted to work on.

It is a pertinent point that for many of the Asian women joining the project, initial discussions focusing on the identification of 'personal needs' failed to find a resonance. Many women could not relate to this topic, nor address it in a personal context. However, by means of a gradual build up of trust in the group, and being assured of confidentiality, over time more and more women started to reflect on their lives, review areas they had previously not felt able to talk about, and articulate personal aspirations.

In relation to the development of employment opportunities, it is also important to highlight that, over the duration of the project, attention was paid to developing a strategy for tackling external barriers to employment. Publicising the work of the project was a major part of this strategy, as was disseminating information on mental health issues. It was acknowledged that this strategy would need the commitment of additional resources and the further development of the strategy over time.

With regard to service-user participation, as discussed, service users were supported to fully participate in project management board meetings, and in the evaluation and concomitant development of the project. Many service users initially wanted to be accompanied to meetings by advocates who had been pre-briefed by the service user on key issues. The way in which the project management board was conducted also changed, to reflect practices the service users wanted to incorporate. The project management board had never utilised a formal business style, but meetings became even more flexible and informal as a result of service-user involvement, although service users were keen that the meetings should keep to the agreed time-frame. The agenda was also always open, so that anyone involved with the project could highlight an area to be discussed. It also had to be borne in mind that not all service users wanted extended involvement and that encouragement to participate had to be broached sensitively to ensure that service users did not experience this encouragement as unwelcome addition-al pressure. With regard to the project, those service users who did not want to become project management board members, regularly fed their views on the project into project management board meetings by means of impact interviews with the project evaluator, or discussions with workers, service-user representatives or advocates. In line with the objective of 'further developing service-user participation in the initiative', it was also possible to work with other groups on the establishment of service-user forums with a wider-ranging brief. It was recognised that, over time, these forums would require ongoing resourcing and support. It was also acknowledged that the ways in which the forums informed existing planning bodies would also require further attention.

Effective links with other agencies were initiated at the outset of the project and built on throughout. Agencies were keen to look at how the project involved service users and the 'action evaluation' framework was viewed both positively and enthusiastically. Agency workers in particular found the 'action evaluation' an informative, non-threatening means of providing information for managers, policy-makers and themselves on how their service was operating, and to press for more resources.

The aspect of the programme focusing on culturally appropriate and eth-nically sensitive training proved perhaps to be the most controversial, given the variations in emphasis during the 1990s and later in the United Kingdom on 'cultural awareness training' and 'anti-racist training'. The sessions emphasised anti-oppressive and anti-discriminatory practice, as well as focusing on aspects highlighted as important by those working in the field. The evaluation of the training programme resulted in the production of a 'good practice' guide. Key points included the importance of ensuring that training on 'race' and mental health is incorporated into mainstream training programmes, rooted in broad equal opportunities policies, and is continuous, rather than one-off and tokenistic; that professionals and service users from ethnic communities fully participate in the planning and operation of training programmes; and that the particular needs of participants on the training pro-grammes and the ethnic mix are considered carefully . These aspects are not new, and have been highlighted by, among others, CCETSW (1993) and

Sayce (2000). Sayce, in particular, advocates holding sessions for mixed groups of staff, users/survivors and family members, enabling participants to see issues from a number of different viewpoints.

Conclusion

This chapter has focused on the carrying out of an 'action evaluation' which had an inclusive brief. It was not fully user-led, but clarified what participation meant, and emphasised the importance of drawing up ethical statements at the outset so that all those involved knew what they could expect, and what would be expected from them. The project met all of the long-term outcomes linked to each of the objectives. In this sense, the evaluative framework can be seen to have determined the success of the project with realistic objectives and outcomes being devised and amended in line with changed circumstances and resources. Documenting the changes made, and the reasons for these, as the project progressed, also served to keep a record of process information. This proved to be invaluable, not only in terms of ensuring that lessons were learned from the evaluation which could inform 'action evaluations' carried out elsewhere, but also in terms of justifying changes to the funding body.

Overall, it is possible to assert that the 'action evaluation' was positively rated as a form of evaluation. Service-user involvement and participation in the evaluative process were commended. The ongoing production of accessible and utilisable information was also particularly praised. Additionally, this form of 'action evaluation' demonstrated the advantage of inbuilt flexibility in that it can be used in line with the specified framework, or it can be developed and built on to address specifically the features of the project, initiative or service being evaluated.

Notes

1.   It is important to emphasise that the term 'Asian' is used to refer to diverse groupings of men and women from different ethnic communities.

References

Barnes, C and Mercer, G *Doing Disability Research* Leeds, Disability Press

Beresford, P.and Trevillion, S (1995) *Developing Skills for Community Care: A collaborative approach* Aldershot, Arena

CCETSW (1993) *Improving Mental Health Practice: A training manual* Leeds, Northern Curriculum Development project Anti-Racist Social Work Education

Cheetham, J, Fuller, R, Mc Ivor, G and Petch, A (1992) *Evaluating Social Work Effectiveness* Buckingham, Open University Press

Evans, C and Fisher, M (1999) 'Collaborative evaluation with service users' in Shaw, I and Lishman, J (1999) (eds) *Evaluation and Social Work Practice* London, Sage

Faulkner, A and Layzell, S (2000) *Strategies for Living: A report of user-led research into people's strategies for living with mental distress* London, Mental Health Foundation

Fawcett, B (2000) *Feminist Perspectives on Disability* Harlow, Prentice Hall

Fulbright-Anderson, K, Kubish, A C and Connell, J (1998) 'New approaches to evaluating community initiatives' in *Theory, Measurement and Analysis*, Vol. 2, New York, Aspen Institute

Hart, E and Bond, M (1995) *Action Research for Health and Social Care* Buckingham, Open University Press

Moore, M, Beazley, S and Maelzer, J (1998) *Researching Disability* Buckingham, Open University Press

Nuffield Foundation Community Care Division (1996) *User Perspectives on Research* Leeds, Nuffield

Pawson, R and Tilley, N (1997) *Realistic Evaluation* London, Sage

Sayce, L (2000) *From Psychiatric Patient to Citizen: Overcoming Discrimination and Social Exclusion* Basingstoke, Palgrave

Shaw, I and Lishman, J (1999) (eds) *Evaluation and Social Work Practice* London, Sage

Wagner, L, Ford, R, Bagnall, S, Morgan, S, McDaid, C and Mawhinney, S (1998) *Down Your Street: Models of Extended Community Support Services for People with Mental Health Problems* London, Sainsbury Centre

CHAPTER 6
Towards Resettlement in the Community: Users' Hopes and Fears
Judy Dean, Jeanette Harding and Hannah Morrow

There is an increasing willingness among statutory providers to involve mental health users in planning new services. This involvement has not extended to users remaining in long-stay hospitals, who too often are defined and described in terms of their disabilities, and rarely by their strengths or uniqueness as individuals. This is the story of our experiences, as project manager, group advocate and user interviewer. What follows is a description of our research work, the opportunities that arose from it, the obstacles we faced during it, and others we continue to face now that we are implementing the findings.

Local Background and Context
In 1996/7 the then Cambridge and Huntingdon Health Authority (CHHA) undertook a review of the Cambridge Psychiatric Rehabilitation Service (CPRS), which culminated in a local strategy recommending both service and cultural changes. Part of this strategy required the Trust to ascertain whether any current inpatients of their rehabilitation service could be discharged and resettled into more suitable community accommodation. They stated that the resettlement of 14 people would enable one of the wards, deemed to be environmentally unsuitable, to be closed. Moreover, they stated explicitly:

> It is a cardinal principle that users and their advocates can and should contribute to the progressive transformation of services in ways which reflect their hopes and aspirations (CHHA, 1998).

Capitalising on the explicit reference to user involvement and advocacy, we (the Trust's project manager and the group advocate) secured funding from the Health Authority to employ users to interview their peers in hospital, in order to ascertain their views about their lives in hospital and their aspirations for the future.

Employing users as researchers was a way of challenging directly the paternalistic service culture identified by the CHHA in its review, and enhancing the validity of our work; growing evidence from the literature suggests that users are able to elicit more honest responses through their shared experience, equality of status and independence from the mental health system.

In addition, the Trust's project manager, as part of her M.A. in Mental Health at Anglia Polytechnic University, was keen to include an evaluation of this participatory approach, given that it had not been tested previously within the Trust (Dean, 2001)

Aims of the project

Collectively, we were aware of being faced with a large and challenging task, but had a clear vision. Our aims were:

- To canvass the views and aspirations of users in hospital in a way that recognised their strengths and uniqueness;
- To inform them of resettlement plans;
- To evaluate the benefit of involving users in the research process;
- To evaluate whether the project had influenced staff attitudes; and
- To promote user involvement within the Trust.

The focus on strengths underpinned the work, and was demonstrated in the research process itself:

- Users were involved in formulating the research questions and developing the interview schedule;
- Users were employed to undertake all interviews and were viewed as experts by experience;
- Users were expected to arrange their own interviews, manage their own workloads and finish interviews within a specified timeframe;
- The questions asked focused on users' unique history, capabilities, interests and future wishes, and not on pathology;
- Users were interviewed at a time and pace that suited their individual circumstances;
- User interviewers were involved in analysing the data and writing up findings; and
- Dissemination of findings involved interviewers presenting in a range of forums to a wide audience.

Guiding values

Before describing the project in greater detail we want first to summarise the values that have been fundamental in shaping the research, and continue to be important in driving the work forward. The value base has its roots within Social Role Valorisation (Wolfensberger, 1983) and the Strengths Approach (Rapp and Wintersteen, 1989):

- All people have the potential to learn, grow and develop;
- Users have unique life histories, and inherent human and social value;

- Users in hospital should be afforded dignity and rights irrespective of their levels of performance or difficulties;
- Users may have disabilities and deficiencies, but this is not the sum of their person – they also possess skills and talents;
- Important knowledge can be gleaned from the subjective experience of users, who should be viewed as experts about themselves;
- Users should be well informed in order to make choices and have the freedom to make mistakes; and
- Users have the right to support in order to maintain their autonomy and, in times of need, to be dependent on others.

In the resettlement context, proponents of these values see long-term hospitalisation as an inherently damaging experience for users and a major obstacle to the fulfilment of socially valued roles. Ramon (1991) states:

People stop being mothers/fathers, wives/husbands, sons/daughters, friends, workers, citizens, charming or nasty; they are "patients".

Assessment in the context of resettlement

The traditional methods of assessing potential for resettlement are another example of mental health practice which largely disempowers users. The literature review revealed how standardised rating scales used to measure and score users' disabilities have been the main assessment tools used to determine suitability to leave hospital. Moreover, rather than seeking users' own views about their preferences for future housing and community support, front-line care staff have been the main informants. Medical case notes are also used, though these are criticised for inaccuracy, incompleteness and superficiality in reducing an individual's history and ongoing experience to signs and symptoms of mental illness (Ingleby,1981; Perring, 1992).

There are good examples of user-centred assessments, however. Developed in the field of learning disability, the 'getting to know you' approach has also been applied successfully in mental health (Braisby *et al.*, 1988). The user interview schedule we developed was also influenced by two user self-assessment tools: the Avon Mental Health Measure developed by MIND, and Alan Leader's 'Direct Power' (1995).

Laying the foundations for the research

Initially, our time was spent gaining ownership of the process. We formed a small project group consisting of the Social Services' mental health team manager, head psychologist of the rehabilitation service, and two of the authors (project manager and group advocate). This group met regularly for the duration of the project, and reported back progress at the operational and strategic levels outlined in Figure 6.1.

The views of users on the wards were canvassed to find out how best to conduct the research in the hospital, and to sound out our ideas about employing users as researchers. The project manager recruited two staff from each of the five wards to act as communication links and facilitators of the process.

Figure 6.1 Communication Structure

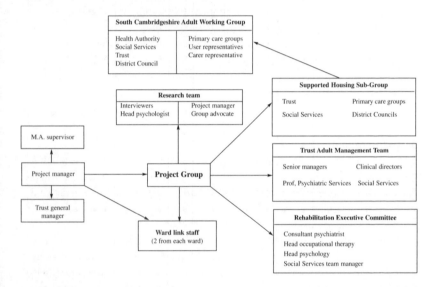

The research project
There were three distinct pieces of research work that have informed this chapter:

(i)   The hospital user project;
(ii) The user interviewer evaluation; and
(iii) The link staff evaluation

Table 6.1 summarises the research methodology and the differing levels of user involvement for each:

Table 6.1 Summary details of research methodology and process

	Hospital User Project	User Interviewer Evaluation	Link Staff Evaluation
Interviewee details	• 50 users on 5 rehabilitation wards: 33 men and 17 women • Average age 44 • 4 from ethnic minorities • 9 detained under the Mental Health Act • Average stay in hospital 8 years	• 5 users living in the community: 2 women and 3 men	• 9 staff working on the 5 rehabilitation wards
Method and type of data collection	• Schedule structured interviews using pre-printed schedule • Qualitative and Quantitative data	• Focused interviews • Qualitative data	• Focused interviews • Qualitative data
Who developed the research tools?	• Project manager and group advocate • Consultation with hospitalised users on methodology • Interview schedule amended by user researchers	• User researchers • Group advocate	• Project manager
Who collected the data?	• User researchers • Group advocate	• 2 of the user researchers	• Project manager
Where was the data collected	• On the wards where they lived	• In the interviewers' homes	• On the wards where they worked
Who analysed the data	• Project manager and group advocate with two of the user researchers. Project manager undertook a further in-depth thematic and qualitative analysis for M.A dissertation.	• One of the user researchers and Project manager	• Project manager
Where was the information disseminated	• Interviewees (written feedback via research team) • Link staff and ward teams • Housing sub-group • Trust management group • Conference presentations: verbal and posters (research team) • M.A. dissertation	• Link staff • Poster presentation at Community Nurse Conference (research team) • Regional Conference, National Schizophrenia Fellowship • M.A. dissertation	• Link staff • M.A. dissertation

Recruitment of interviewers

User interviewers were recruited by the group advocate who had previous experience of supporting users in fulfilling positive roles in the community, and was able to publicise opportunities for user interviewers and interviewees, and encourage their involvement. As a user-focused organisation, the advocacy service's involvement helped to reassure them that the project would be user-focused, and its outcomes would be in their best interests.

Initially, eight users expressed an interest in being involved, with five eventually completing training and undertaking interviews. All five had a long history of contact with services; three since adolescence. Two interviewers had direct experience of the wards where interviews took place.

Interviewer training

The project group developed a training and support package for the nine-month duration of the project. Interviewers attended three full days, four half-day sessions and a site visit to meet staff and potential interviewees prior to the interviews commencing.

Training was held in a community hall, with breaks taken every hour, free lunch and refreshments. Brainstorming and role-play were the main training methods used, to enable the team to get to know one other. Table 6.2 outlines the three-day programme. The half days focused entirely on the practical use of the interview schedule. Interviewers took turns to adopt interviewer and interviewee roles, and were asked to play out a range of different situations. These sessions were followed by debriefing, where interviewers were asked to reflect on how they had felt.

Table 6.2   User interviewer training programme

	Morning	Afternoon
Day 1	Introductions Getting to know each other Project presentation Hopes, fears and expectations	Interviewing skills: ● self presentation ● setting up environment ● building rapport/active listening
Day 2	Touching base Interviewing skills: ● Handling difficult situations The Perceptions of others (interviewees and ward staff-identifying potential obstacles)	Introducing the interview schedule Recording the interview Ethics (gaining consent/confidentiality)
Day 3	Meeting ward link staff Meeting Sainsbury Centre user interviewers	Role playing the use of the interview schedule

The rationale behind inviting user interviewers from the Sainsbury Centre was twofold: to share experiences and thereby instil confidence in the group; and to demonstrate to staff that participatory research was supported by a renowned organisation.

Interviewer support
> *There was one person who was in the adolescent unit with me in the 1970s and I know he has been in hospital ever since then. I felt quite sad about that.*

Weekly research team meeting
Group meetings were held in interviewers' own homes, with a shared lunch, and lasted at least an hour. These forums served different functions and were evaluated positively by all the interviewers:

- *Providing debriefing support and encouragement*: sharing feelings evoked from interviews;
- *General information exchange*: about the project, research team members' news, how interviews had gone;
- *Problem solving*: overcoming resistance of staff/interviewee refusals/covering interviewer sickness;
- *Planning interviewer workload for the week*: taking account of other work/personal priorities; and
- *Administration*: collection of completed interviews/issuing new schedules/payment.

We cannot overestimate the importance of these group meetings. They were crucial for emotional support, practical management and monitoring the progress of the project.

The trust and friendships that developed within the group also meant that it was safe to share personal experience of the mental health system:

> *We really looked forward to our weekly meeting. It very quickly became a close knit group. Some of us shared past traumatic experiences of being an inpatient. We had never done this before.*

In addition to the weekly research team meetings, interviewers were also offered telephone support, but apart from a few occasions early on, interviewers did not use this.

Written authorisation
During training, interviewers expressed concern about accessing interviewees in the event of meeting unfamiliar staff who would be unaware of their role. A letter legitimising access, written by the project manager and group advocate, was carried by interviewers, though they were never required to show it.

Interviewer introductions

During training, interviewers were assisted in drawing up an introductory statement covering:

- Details about themselves and their experience of services;
- The aims of the project;
- Confidentiality; and
- What would happen to the information interviewers gave.

Although utilised in early interviews as an aide memoire and to combat nerves, its use declined as interviewers grew in confidence.

Interviewer payment

The Trust's finance manager was supportive in setting up the system for interviewer payments. Interviewers were paid £20 for each completed interview, plus £5 for their written summary of the interview, which was sent to interviewees. This was paid at a rate of £15 per week in cash, so that welfare benefits were unaffected. Despite being a somewhat arduous administrative task for the project manager, this system meant that users did not have to wait for payment.

Main findings

Of the 58 users who were approached for interview, 50 were completed successfully, with interviews taking an hour on average.

Perceptions of hospital life

Hospital life was seen by the majority as a negative experience, Table 6.3 summarises users' responses:

Table 6.3   Perceptions of hospital life

Themes	Number of users	Positive aspects	Negative aspects
Staff relationships	31	Feeling valued, cared about and enjoyed staff company	Social distancing, feeling devalued, being coerced and controlled. Not feeling listened to, given insufficient staff time
Meaning of hospital	29	Security, convalescence, freedom from responsibility	Boredom, illness-creating, like a prison (a place for punishment, atonement or entrapment), futile, lack of opportunity to pursue interests
Physical environment	23	Tranquil grounds	Distance from town, lack of privacy, poor facilities, smoking
Peer relationship	23	Empathy, friendship	Harassment, shared/forced living accommodation
Freedom	21	None identified	Restriction of movement, rules and routines, lack of access to own money
Personal identity	20	None identified	Loss of valued roles, poverty, loss of confidence, estrangement from friends and family

The social distancing noted as a negative aspect was also observed by inter-viewers, who reported that users had told them that, despite years of hospitalisation, this was the first time they had been asked to tell their story.

Strengths and talents
The majority of users (92 per cent) were able to identify a range of skills and talents. Many felt that their personal attributes had helped them to cope with their hospital experience and their relationships with others, both staff and peers. Some were engaged in self-directed study, while others attempted to pursue hobbies within their limited financial resources. For the majority, however, it appeared that their skills were unrecognised and had become obsolete in the hospital setting.

Community aspirations
The majority of users (72 per cent) wanted to leave hospital and live indepen-dently with varying levels of practical support. Only 20 per cent wanted hospital staff to support them in the community, and only 18 per cent wanted to live with or near others from the hospital. Users also chose mainstream community facilities above mental health specific day care.

Given these aspirations, we found that an alarming 64 per cent of users leave the hospital grounds less than once weekly. For those not legally detained, apprehensiveness, a lack of staff support and little available money were cited as reasons.

Perceived benefits of leaving hospital included increased freedom and independence, being able to find voluntary or paid work, and an opportunity to build new relationships and renew old contacts. Many users also felt their self-perception would improve.

The impact on users, interviewers and staff
   It has been useful in that it lets people know what I'm like as a person.
   It's important that I'm not stereotyped as a mentally-ill person.

The majority of users welcomed the opportunity to talk about their lives in a supportive and unhurried way, without fear of judgement. Accounts of domestic violence, having children taken into care and exploitation in the workplace, although difficult for interviewers to listen to, resulted in greater understanding and empathy. For some users, it was the first time they had spoken about their lives before hospital, and this served to reinforce the importance of the interviewer role in giving users a voice.

Reflecting on individuals stories resulted in interviewers reappraising their own mental health service experiences, and an increased insight into the impact of long-term hospitalisation. With this greater understanding came not only a respect and admiration for the resilience shown by those they interviewed, but also a new motivation and sense of purpose for themselves.

Despite thinking it was a good idea in theory to employ users, staff were sceptical about how successful interviewers would be in gleaning information from residents. Staff thought that some would be incapable of expressing themselves and would be reluctant to talk to someone they did not know. This paternalism also extended to interviewers, whose ability to carry out the work was also questioned; concern was expressed about how they would cope with rejection, or being reminded of their own hospital experiences.

All link staff had anticipated the need to offer emotional support to both interviewees and interviewers immediately prior to/following an interview, yet in reality this support was rarely sought. On the contrary:

There was a lot of talk after each interview and the residents would say "Oh, we've talked about this and it was really good and he was a really nice bloke." I've never seen them respond so well in such a positive way to any other interviews they have had.

Users felt that inquiring about strengths and future aspirations, although of critical importance to them, were rarely explored by staff. Sharing this information empowered interviewees and instilled confidence and hope for the future, despite interviewers being clear that no promises could be made.

The majority of users consented to staff having a copy of their interview feedback. Most of this information was new to staff, and all stated their intention to utilise it within care planning. It has been heartening for us to witness many positive changes as a direct result of our work, although there is still much to do.

The quality and type of information that interviewers obtained challenged directly the view that users could not/did not have clear views, as well as serving to reinforce users' strengths and skills, as both interviewees and interviewers. It also led staff to conclude that users speaking to users, rather than to staff, elicit more honest responses.

Staff reflected on what users said about their lives in hospital, and their wish to leave. Some staff vowed to listen more, while others were hurt by users' criticisms and became defensive. However, the knowledge that users desired a better life for themselves culminated in the majority of link staff concluding that they had underestimated users' abilities and potential for life outside hospital:

It amazed me that users who appear so damaged and preoccupied with their auditory hallucinations, and seem to be taking very little interest in anything but their cigarettes and medication, can be talking about

*their future and saying where they would like to live in the community.
I had thought, 'Oh, they will always need to be in the institution', but
maybe they won't be, maybe they can move out.*

Through a similar process of reflection on the process, interviewers reported
a boost in confidence and self-esteem as a direct result of being involved in
work which

*turned our experience of the psychiatric system around from a
negative to a positive one.*

For interviewers, remuneration for the work validated their role and for
most was their first experience of being paid as a user of services. However,
it was not the payment but rather a commitment and belief in the project that
ensured completion of the work and the willingness to be further involved in
implementing the findings.

Obstacles

*I was told on two or three occasions to, well they put it bluntly, "get
knotted"*

The obstacles faced have differed at each stage of the process. Overcoming
some of these have been within our direct control, while others have not.

Research obstacles

Staff paternalism was worrying for some interviewers, but fortunately was
confined to only one ward. One or two staff knew interviewers formerly as
inpatients on the acute wards, and their resistance to the process took the
form of delaying access to the interviewees. Two successful strategies were
employed to overcome this. First, the project manager and one of the interviewers attended a ward meeting to stress the need to work as an alliance,
reassuring staff that interviewers had been trained and were being supported
in the role. Second, the project manager used her personal relationship with
users to facilitate access.

A small minority of users flatly declined an interview. Initially, this disheartened and disappointed interviewers, particularly where this had
happened at their first interview. A more philosophical approach was
adopted over time, with the successful completion of interviews. A few
users did not complete the whole of their interview; they were offered
further opportunities, and interviewers were advised to concentrate on the
section relating to leaving hospital and housing preferences. Interviewers
were flexible enough to reallocate outstanding interviews among themselves when some were having difficulty in completing them within the
time-scale allowed.

Organisational barriers

The project took place in the context of enormous organisational change, which hindered the implementation process considerably:

- Shortly after developing the strategy informing this work, the Health Authority was reconfigured to extend its geography and take in areas with relatively poorly developed mental health services;
- The Acute Trusts' mental health services were in the process of merging to become a county-wide health and social care trust; and
- The publication of the Mental Health National Service Framework has given priority to groups that do not include those on long-stay wards.

Inevitably, change leads to uncertainty, not least in respect of planning future service developments. Implementation within this context has required patience and political acumen.

Where are we now?

The project manager now leads a project implementation group which has agreed a supported living service model. Visits to other services have demonstrated to staff that long-stay users need not live in health-staffed hostels, or in registered care homes, condemning them to low levels of income. Similarly, nurses have witnessed that 'their' users could manage without high levels of trained staff support. The paternalistic views held by medical staff are now a minority view.

The fact that the group advocate and one of the user interviewers are members of the project implementation group has meant that decisions we have made, and will continue to make, take account of users' expressed wishes. We are all members of the strategic South Cambridgeshire Adult Working Group (see 6.1) that will ensure the project maintains its high profile.

For the interviewers, this work has culminated in new opportunities and increased self-confidence. One now works as a voluntary group advocate within the hospital and, as a qualified aerobics teacher, runs fitness sessions for service users. Another has found paid employment with a local user-led information service and is identified as an 'expert user'. Three of the five are undertaking an NVQ to equip them as user trainers. Others have continued their research interest through involvement in a local review of supported housing, the findings of which, alongside our work, are informing new housing developments.

Concluding remarks

As a direct consequence of employing users as interviewers, we have furthered our knowledge of the plight of users in long-stay wards, and raised their profile locally. We have also influenced care practices positively, and staff attitudes towards a more valuing and optimistic view of those in their care.

For the interviewers themselves, other doors have been opened. With these new endeavours have come opportunities for further empowerment.

Finally, we are determined to ensure that new housing reflects expressed wishes. This will be the final test of our success.

Note

We wish to thank the user interviewers, Robin Cox, Andrew Hall, Chris Novak and Carol Morgan. Without their hard work and commitment this work would have been far less valuable.

References

Braisby, D, Echlin, R, Hill, S and Smith, H (1988) *Changing Futures Housing and support services for people discharged from psychiatric hospitals* London, Kings Fund

CHHA (Cambridge and Huntingdon Health Authority) (1998) *Adult Mental Health Services – Changes and Developments in Rehabilitation and Long Term Care*

Dean, J (2001) 'Ascertaining the views, hopes and wishes of users in hospital – A participatory research approach' M.A. dissertation, Anglia Polytechnic University

Ingleby, D (1981) *Critical Psychiatry: The politics of Mental health* Harmondsworth, Penguin

Leader, A (1995) *Direct Power: A resource pack for people who want to develop their own care plans and support networks* Brighton, Pavilion Publishing

Perring, C (1992) 'The experience and perspectives of patients and care staff on the transition from hospital to community based care' in Ramon, S (ed.) *Psychiatric Hospital Closure* London, Chapman Hall

Ramon, S (1991) *Beyond Community Care* London, Macmillan

Rapp, C and Wintersteen, R (1989) 'The strengths model of case management: Results from twelve demonstrations' *Psychosocial Rehabilitation Journal* 13(1), pp 23–32

Wolfensberger, W (1983) 'Social role valorisation-A proposed new term for the principle of normalisation' *Mental Retardation* 21(6), pp 234–39

CHAPTER 7
Making Sense of Personality Disorder
Heather Castillo and Lesley Allen

We imagine that some readers are asking, 'What kind of person receives a diagnosis of personality disorder?' Frequently the subject of sensational press, personality disorder has attracted its own undesirable mythology which, in turn, has generated both fear and plans for containment. The public and professional debate regarding personality disorder has been largely uninformed by the user perspective. Little attention has been paid to service users with this diagnosis, and the meaning they give to their inner world. This study invites you inside.

The setting for the study was an established advocacy service run by Colchester MIND. During the 1990s, a growing number of disaffected people with the personality disorder diagnosis sought advocacy support from the service in Colchester. However, assistance in finding solutions to their problems was largely ineffective. Some had simply been denied mental health services, others had lost their children via child protection procedures, some had been sent to secure hospitals, and some had ended in prison. In July 1997, a consultant in public health for North Essex Health Authority published an article in the *Guardian* entitled 'Everyone's life has a price'. His suggestion that money could be saved by denying hospital admission to those with personality disorder prompted a local service user to write from hospital stating, 'I am a victim of childhood sexual and ritual abuse. I am not yet a survivor. I don't see why I should be deprived of the care and expert counselling that I most definitely need. It was, after all, not me who carried out abuse on a minor. I am just trying to cope with the aftermath.' By July 1999, the Home Office had issued policy proposals for managing dangerous people with severe personality disorder, suggesting removal to special units, without deterioration in clinical state, if deemed to be potentially dangerous to the public (Department of Health,1999). This seemed to cause fairly widespread fear among those with the diagnosis. The advocacy service began to hear from anxious service users who had at some time received the diagnosis, or who had at one time assaulted another, no matter how minor the offence. Notwithstanding assurances regarding the small number proposed for indeterminate detention and their historical dangerousness, many were not calmed: comments included 'This is doing time for no crime', 'It's the thin end of the wedge'. The impulse to form a local research group arose from a growing and shared sense of alienation among those who had attracted this label.

Our group of 18 service users, all of whom had received the personality disorder diagnosis, met monthly throughout 1999. Our inquiries began with an examination of the history of this diagnosis which, we were to discover, spans 200 years, beginning in 1801 with a French psychiatrist, Pinel, who spoke of 'mania without delirium'. Throughout the nineteenth century, the concept of this condition included terms such as 'moral imbecility, 'degenerative deviation' and 'psychopathic inferiority'. Setting a diagnostic course for the future, in 1885, Henry Maudsley wrote, 'It is not our business, and it is not in our power, to explain psychologically the origins and nature of these depraved instincts, it is sufficient to establish their existence as facts of observation'.

Today, following a tradition of psychiatric observation that is concerned with surface manifestations, European and American diagnostic manuals refer to enduring patterns of behaviour that deviate markedly from the expectations of the individual's culture, and pervasive, inflexible deficits that are stable over time (ICD 10, 1992; DSM IV 1994). This gives the service user little cause for any hope at all. It is a category that does not have much scientific credibility, and it is a diagnosis that is often hidden from patients. This caused Lewis and Appleby (1988) to report, in their study 'Personality disorder: The patients psychiatrists dislike', that untreatability is a widely held belief, and that professionals view such service users as long-term management problems. This prompted Lewis and Appleby to conclude that 'personality disorder appears to be an enduring pejorative judgement rather than a clinical diagnosis'.

When service users are devalued it is difficult for them to question the assumptions of the majority alone. The support of other people who share experiences and perceptions helps to set in motion collective action that may challenge conventional wisdom (Brandon, 1995). A research partnership was therefore created, where the study was managed by the advocacy service of Colchester MIND, and supervised and funded by the School of Community Health and Social Studies at Anglia Polytechnic University.

Although there are 10 diagnostic subcategories attributed to personality disorder, the two most commonly diagnosed are borderline personality disorder and dissocial/anti-social personality disorder. This was reflected in our group, where all members had acquired either a borderline or dissocial diagnosis. Service users with borderline personality disorder are characterised as emotionally unstable, impulsive and self-destructive, while dissocial personality disorder is described as a callous unconcern for others, with deviant social behaviour and a potential for danger to one's fellows.

Therefore, a vital early group decision was whether members with a border-line diagnosis would be willing to include, and feel comfortable about including those with a dissocial diagnosis. This was an important ethical decision, because it might be considered that 'abused' and 'abuser' would be drawn into an unwilling association. Identifying common issues of stigma, discrimination and early life events, the consensus of the group was in favour of inclusion. In fact, *esprit de corps* came easily to this group. Why should this be? After all, some were considered to be 'difficult customers'. Solidarity against the world, perhaps? There were certain hallmarks connected to our group. It was always the same room in which we met: warm; next to the smoking room; with a bottomless supply of tea, coffee and biscuits. Group cohesiveness deepened throughout the year, with much exploration of loss, early history, experiences within the psychiatric system, and common coping strategies. The group was always unstructured. It resisted structure and ambled its way through two hours on Thursday after-noons, yet much was discussed and much was achieved.

Nine group members began to produce stories in order to examine the relationship between life events and their disorder (Brown and Harris, 1989). Some agreed to keep journals; others to write poetry or letters. Five members of the group expressed a wish to be trained as researchers in order to interview 50 people with the diagnosis in the Colchester area. With the help of supervisors, the group set out to create an interview questionnaire. The study used a mixture of qualitative and quantitative methods. The questionnaire began qualitatively, with a semi-structured interview. The group wanted service users to explore and share their experiences; they wanted to show what it really means to receive a diagnosis of personality disorder. They wished to know what the diagnosis meant to service users, how they had discovered they had this diagnosis, how this made them feel, what did they consider were their problems and strengths, what if anything had helped, and, in an ideal world what should services be like? The remainder of the questionnaire was quantitative, with a fixed format that included demographic and diagnostic information, life experiences, symptoms, behaviours, and a rating table for types of support and intervention.

In April 1999, a five-week training programme was launched by the advocacy service manager and supervisors from Anglia Polytechnic University, involving a co-operative inquiry group of service users from Lifecraft in Cambridge. Training included communication and interview skills, ethical issues, good practice, and practical issues concerning timetabling, the environment, support and expenses. It was agreed that researchers would receive a payment of £30 for each interview conducted, and respondents would receive £10 for their participation.

It is important to understand that the researchers were not 'survivors' engaged in a retrospective study, but rather 'sufferers' struggling for emotional equilibrium while engaged in a research endeavour. Consequently, our study was fraught with questions regarding who might relapse next, and ethical dilemmas regarding the stressful nature of our inquiry. Our five researchers reduced to four almost as soon as the training programme began and two more were to be admitted to hospital during the course of the study. All four researchers negotiated very great personal difficulties during this time, yet all continued to contribute to the study once more as soon as they were able. One said, 'if I give up hope on this, then there's nothing left.' Other group members experienced their own individual problems. They still came to join us each month. Some came from the hospital wards. Some came even when 'sectioned'. The commitment was breathtaking.

Once training and pilot work were completed, it was necessary to obtain ethical permission to carry out the study. We were invited to attend a meeting of the local research ethics committee on a warm evening in May. One of the service-user researchers accompanied the advocacy service manager to the meeting. At the entrance she asked 'Do you think I should cover my arms?' On reflection, she did not feel she should have to do so. Bearing the scars of years of self-harm, she sat with some dignity and answered questions articulately and with candour. However, we suspected that such a research proposal might prove an uncomfortable proposition for any research ethics committee. Our suspicions were confirmed, and it took more than three months of negotiations before permission for the study was granted. In the meantime, we launched our research on a self-selected basis involving members of the group. During August, ethical permission was received, but by this time we had already completed fourteen interviews.

After permission was obtained, we followed the guidance of the ethics committee by contacting seven local consultant psychiatrists with details of our study and asked for suggested respondents. However, although the psychiatrists were very co-operative in other ways, causing no delays and not refusing access to any of their patients, they suggested very few respondents for the study: three in all. By late November, we had completed forty interviews. Respondents had been accessed almost entirely through the networking activities of the advocacy service and the group. Only two had refused to be interviewed. Such a high response rate might be viewed as a testament to the support service users were willing to give to other service users involved in research. The voluntary sector rallied support in the last few weeks, helping us to access the remaining 10 interviewees. Nineteen interviews were conducted in respondents' homes, eighteen in hospital, nine were carried out at the MIND Social Centre or nearby voluntary centres, and four responded by mail, including two who had recently moved out of the area, one from an out-of-area secure unit, and the fourth wrote from prison. By 20 December 1999, the last interview had been carried out. The sample of 50 was now complete.

Capturing the voice of the sample, the study yielded an abundance of service-user perspectives, and the completed research report was to include almost 15,000 client words (Castillo, 2000). The study consisted of interviews with 50 people, 40 per cent of whom were men, and 60 per cent women. Ages ranged between 18 and 74. The majority of interviewees – 86 per cent, were aged between 25 and 54. Eighty-six per cent were single, divorced or separated, and 66 per cent were living alone. Eighty-eight per cent were on long-term sickness or other benefits. Just one was full-time employed. Fifty-eight per cent had a diagnosis of borderline personality disorder, for 28 per cent it was dissocial, and for the remaining fourteen per cent their personality disorder diagnosis was unspecified. An analysis of additional psychiatric diagnoses showed that 78 per cent had a diagnosis of depression and 60 per cent of anxiety. Eighty-six per cent of service users in this study described their difficulties in terms of depression or anxiety, and often combinations of both. So, why should they have received a diagnosis of personality disorder? Four interviewees had recently received a re-diagnosis of bipolar or mood disorder. All four were articulate and not slow to express their grievances. It may be that they had originally received a diagnosis of personality disorder because they were perceived as trouble-makers. However, a question existed, was there a link among the remainder? The findings revealed a correlation in terms of early trauma and often brutal life experiences. Eighty-eight per cent had suffered abuse, violent, sexual and/or emotional, and for 80 per cent this was childhood abuse.

There exists extensive support for the concept of a complex post-traumatic syndrome in survivors of prolonged and repeated victimisation (Herman, 1992; Van der Kolk, 1996; Fonagy, 1997). Behaviour manifestations of self-mutilation, re-victimisation, victimising others, dissociative disorders, substance abuse and eating disorders, employed as strategies aimed at regaining internal equilibrium, have been discovered in victims of early trauma. This suggests a tendency, in later life, to cope with thoughts and feelings through physical action: 'Do it either to my body or to your body'. Not being able to find themself from within, individuals are forced to find a sense of self from the outside by treating themselves as an object, or by getting others to react to them. The findings of our study concurred in that 88 per cent had engaged in self-harming activities such as cutting, overdosing or self-starvation; 76 per cent had engaged in alcohol or drug misuse; and 82 per cent had attempted suicide.

Irvine Goffman (1961) examined the 'moral career' of the service user in the context of identity. Here, the process of development can be followed by studying moral experiences and personal adjustments. An 'alteration of social fate' begins for our sample with the revelation that a diagnosis of personality disorder has been conferred. The reaction to this new-found knowledge included 'anger, feeling insulted, blamed, depressed, anxious, daft, abnormal, numb, bewildered, helpless, shocked, and excluded'. Confirming that the diagnosis is stigmatising, service users described being treated as a 'services leper'. Others said 'you're ignored', that the label 'arouses hostility' that it was 'brought on oneself', that 'people seem to be scared of the diagnosis', or 'it's saying troublemaker'. Many discovered indirectly that they had the diagnosis, from records, reports or at meetings. Others appear to have been told after many years; and yet others were informed by professionals only after they asked. The sense of exclusion and hopelessness expressed by respondents on making this discovery gives some insight into the impact the information might have on an individual already labouring with the desperately hard task of living with the truth of an early abusive history (Castillo *et al.*, 2001): 'We already feel subhuman, threatened and vulnerable, and now we are tarred with the brush of being bad as well as mad'.

Twenty per cent of women in the study, and 22 per cent of men, had been violent to others. More than 75 per cent of women had received a borderline diagnosis, and over 75 per cent of the men a dissocial diagnosis. None of the men with a borderline diagnosis had been violent to others. Thirty-five per cent of the women with a borderline diagnosis had engaged in violent acts yet had retained the borderline categorisation. Does this suggest that violence in men might attract a diagnosis of psychopathy more easily than for women? Does it highlight the greater likelihood of a prison disposal on the basis of gender? Certainly, 26 per cent of men in our study had experienced being in prison, compared to 12 per cent of women. Fifty per cent of the men with a dissocial diagnosis considered their strengths to be care and compassion. Rather than the stereotypical notion of the psychopath viewing fellow human beings as 'empty vessels', they characterised themselves as 'Jekyll and Hyde', an embodiment of both compassion and aggression. They highlighted the fact that aggression has a context, and that strengths may go unrecognised. Whether the categorisation is borderline or dissocial, our study shows high incidences of early abuse, self-harm and suicidality across categories. Women with a dissocial diagnosis in our study all had a history of early emotional abuse, but none had a history of childhood violence, yet 67 per cent had been violent to others. Where men had experienced early violent abuse, some went on to harm others, and some engaged in self-harm. These findings suggest that violence does not necessarily beget violence, but that early, unresolved and unassimilated trauma can result in the perpetration of harm. This may be directed inwards as self-harm, or outwards as harm to others. This questions the validity of the diagnosis of personality disorder and the subcategories within it.

In this study, service users have proclaimed that 'when you are abused as a child your life is murdered'. Self-states had resulted in suicide attempts of such lethality that survival seemed miraculous. One group member threw herself down a sheer 40ft. cliff face. 'It's amazing how many people try to kill themselves and fail. I feel that even God does not want me.' Anger had become dammed up behind a narrow response function. Words had been cut into flesh. Etched in red against the background of a beautiful young arm was the word '*hate*'. Where early life had been sexually or violently abusive, or simply included an unloving, profoundly humiliating and devastating non-response from caregivers, the blunt limitations of their experience had left some stripped of control and disempowered beyond belief.

An analysis of what helped most revealed that service users seem to be saying understanding and acceptance will get professionals half-way there. The most often reported, and unpopular, professional response in this study was to be told one is 'attention seeking'. To say that someone is attention seeking is to imply that the person is not worthy of attention. It is dismissive. Behaviour can be a form of communication, and the ways in which the system responds to this behaviour may also be dysfunctional. Professionals might rather see behaviours such as self-harm, continual neediness and suicide attempts as 'attachment seeking', which might be better understood in terms of attachment theory and separation anxiety (Bowlby, 1988). The findings include service-user observations about a wide variety of therapeutic interventions. Cognitive analytic therapy (Ryle, 1997) received the highest therapy rating in our study: 'I've seen him [the therapist] for over a year. He's done more than the whole services put together.'

As far as we are aware, this is the first study of its kind where service users have become equal partners engaged specifically in researching a clinical diagnosis (Ramon *et al.*, 2001). Employing an emancipatory research approach, the service users diagnosed with personality disorder have replaced 'the view from above' with 'the view from below' (Freire, 1970). Here, the research tools have been given to the people, and with them they have presented a new construct for consideration which points overwhelmingly to the need for a redefinition of this diagnosis into a category which more clearly suggests aetiology and offers a better understanding of this human condition.

From the perspective of those of us involved in this study, the experience has indeed been emancipating. It has given us a voice and an opportunity to put forward our side of the story and tell people how it really feels. This is an opportunity we have made the most of: we are proud to say that eight articles about our research have been published in national journals, and half of those were co-authored by service users involved in our study. We have presented the results of the research at eighteen conferences. Five of these were high-profile national conferences where, often with shaky legs and trembling voices, we have spoken our truth on platforms shared with some of the most famous names in the field: for once in our traumatic lives we have felt valued and respected. Slowly we are seeing a shift in the views of some professionals, who no longer see personality disorders as untreatable and are helping to develop excellent long-term programmes which are increasingly proving that this is not the case. As for the group, we reformed in February 2001. We still meet monthly and now publish a news sheet which has national circulation. Some of us have moved on, got married, managed to get our children back, have started academic courses, have even begun part-time work. But others still struggle badly. So the work continues.

References

Bowlby, J (1988) *A Secure Base* London, Routledge

Brandon, D (1991) *Innovation Without Change?: Consumer power in psychiatric services*, London, Macmillan

Brown, G and Harris, T (1989) *Life Events and Illness* London, Unwin Hyman

Castillo, H (2000) *Temperament or Trauma? A co-operative inquiry by service users into the nature and treatment of personality disorder* Chelmsford and Cambridge, Anglia Polytechnic University

Castillo, H, Allen, L and Coxhead, N (2001) 'The hurtfulness of a diagnosis: Uuser research about personality disorder' *Mental Health Practice*, 4 (9) pp 16–9

Department of Health (1999) *Managing Dangerous People with Severe Personality Disorder* Home Office Proposals for Policy Development, London, HMSO

DSM IV (1994) *Diagnostic and Statistical Manual of Mental Disorders* (4th edn) Washington DC, American Psychiatric Association

Fonagy, P (1997) *When Cure is Inconceivable: The aims of psychoanalysis with borderline patients* Paper, New York Freudian Society 4 April

Freire, P (1970) *Pedagogy of the Oppressed* New York, Herder and Herder

Goffman, E (1961) *Asylums: Essays on the social situation of mental patients and other inmates* London, Penguin

Herman, J (1992) 'Complex post traumatic stress disorder: a syndrome in survivors of prolonged and repeated trauma' *Journal of Traumatic Stress*, 5, pp 377–92; quoted in Van der Kolk, *Traumatic Stress* London and New York, Guilford

ICD 10 (1992) *Classification of Mental and Behavioural Disorders* Geneva, World Health Organisation

Lewis, G and Appleby, L (1988) 'Personality disorder: the patients psychiatrists dislike' *British Journal of Psychiatry*, 153, pp 44–9

Maudsley, H (1885) *Responsibility in Mental Disease* London, Kegan Paul

Pinel (1801) *Oxford Textbook of Psychiatry* (2nd edn) (ref Kauka, 1949, for translation) Gelder, Gath & Mayou, Oxford Medical Publications, Oxford

Ramon, S, Castillo, H and Morant, N (2001) 'Experiencing personality disorder' *International Journal of Social Psychiatry*

Ryle, A (1997) *Cognitive Analytic Therapy: The model and the method* Chichester, Wiley

Van der Kolk, B (1996) *Traumatic Stress* London and New York, Guilford

CHAPTER 8
Researching User Empowerment in Practice:
Lessons from the Field
Tim Schafer

This chapter explores my experience and the learning gained from my involvement in completing a research project as a part-time Ph.D. student. The project was undertaken within the context of full-time employment as a lecturer whose main responsibility is in teaching the Community Mental Health Nursing Specialist Practice course. The project was ultimately successful in that it has produced some good-quality research data, and has developed knowledge and evidence around the promotion of user empowerment. The promotion of user involvement in the research has been a fundamental value of the project, but the achievement of this has not been without its difficulties. This chapter gives an honest account of the process and the lessons that have been learnt, so that current and future researchers may learn from this experience.

The research focus
The project began to take shape in the mid 1990s, fuelled first by my desire for academic advancement and credibility, and second, by my interest in the notion of 'empowerment' that at that time was being cited as a fundamental practice value and used to justify a range of practices in mental health care. My reading of the literature and personal experiences of empowerment in a self-help context promoted an increasingly critical view of the concept, for the following reasons:

- The commonly-voiced professional view that empowerment was something that was done to, or gifted to, others did not fit my own personal experiences. 'Power comes from within, you can facilitate it, but you can't make it happen' (Wallcraft, 1994);

- Examination of the literature revealed a variety of perspectives, with many contradictory views and opinions. It is a contested concept (Taylor *et al.*, 1992); and

- Increasing personal awareness of general usage of the concept indicated the notion of empowerment being used to justify both right-wing and left-wing policies. The manipulative and social control potential of the concept was exemplified in Ward and Mullender's (1992) paper, where it was described as a "social aerosol" covering up the disturbing smell of conflict and conceptual division'.

My increasingly critical perspective, coupled with increasing recognition given to users in the research process, demanded that the process of the research should promote user empowerment. Relationships were developed with the advocacy workers at the study site, and a research steering group was set up to plan the research aims and processes. The group included advocacy workers, service users, service managers and clinical audit personnel. The most important meeting, where the project seemed to take shape, and commitment from user representatives to the process was assured, took place in a pub in Scarborough outside a MIND conference!

The main requirement of the research for service users and former service users was that it should aim to make a difference in the experiences of people locally, and participatory action research was chosen as a design and value as it promotes change and is particularly suited to the self-help context (Chesler, 1991). The principles of co-operative inquiry were also adopted in many of the processes in the project, though users were not trained or used as researchers, rendering the approach similar to what Heron (1996) describes as a 'weak' form of the research.

Research questions and methods

[I]f the researchers are not themselves the respondents, then the con-clusions will be 'truths' that hang in a curious void – alienated from the values of the researchers, and from the actual and different values of the respondents. (Heron, 1981)

The first phase of the research asked these questions of local service users: 'What does user empowerment mean to us?' and 'What aspects of our care have either helped or hindered this process?' The questions were inves-tigated through the use of individual interviews with advocacy workers, all of whom have experienced services, and focus group interviews with a day-hospital-based 'empowerment' group, a day-hospital user group, and a community-based user group. In addition, I joined the local patients' council as a participant observer for more than six months. The data was analysed using principles of thematic analysis (Tesch, 1990), and process models of disempowerment and empowerment were formulated and agreed. A defini-tion of empowerment was developed, forming the conceptual base for the further investigation in the second phase of the project. The interview and observation schedules were developed through discussion with the advocacy workers and 'empowerment' group. All transcripts were checked by infor-mants for accuracy, and the definition and model development was sent to all contributors to be discussed, amended and agreed. Although service users did not work directly as data collectors, the involvement in the planning of interviews and the validation of the work went a considerable way to ensuring that the conceptual basis of the work was firmly grounded in the values of the participants. The agreed definition of empowerment is reproduced in Box 1.

Box 1:   Definition of 'empowerment'

- Becoming 'empowered' is an ongoing, progressive process whereby individuals develop greater control and responsibility over important aspects of their lives.

- It is characterised by a desire to learn and develop that is grounded in a developing appetite to experience the richness and diversity of life.

- It involves taking on new understandings of experiences and dependencies at the personal, interpersonal and broader social levels.

- Sensitivity to broader social and cultural constraints and opportunities develop, with the focus of problem-solving moving from inside to outside the individual.

- It involves movement from victim towards victor, helpless recipient towards valued giver, from isolation towards integration, and from unhelpful towards helpful dependencies.

The second phase of the project involved the development and administration of two questionnaires. Although the limits of quantitative research are well documented, the survey method helped to supplement and extend the qualitative phase, and considerably widened user involvement and influence. The first questionnaire provides a user-focused evaluation of the caring environment and process, focusing on empowering aspects of the environment. This questionnaire is called the Environment Empowerment Evaluation (EEE) and consists of 39 statements in a Likert scale. The second questionnaire, the Individual Empowerment Assessment (IEA), is a 26-item scale that aims to capture an individual's sense of empowerment. Both scales were developed through an ethnographic content analysis (Altheide, 1987) of the transcripts and field notes that essentially asked the questions, 'How would you know if you were empowered?' and 'What experiences of receiving services have helped or hindered your empowerment?' Many items on the scales are taken directly from the transcripts. The items and scales were developed and piloted by members of the 'empowerment' group over a period of about three months.

The questionnaires were then administered to users in five different care contexts in the locality on two occasions, the second administration taking place a year after the first. The second administration was undertaken so that any trends or differences could be identified, helping users and staff in the areas to evaluate progress, or otherwise. The areas were chosen to capture service users with a wide range of dependencies and difficulties, and included two admission wards, a rehabilitation ward, a self-help 'empowerment' group, and a community-based 'clubhouse'.

The imperative to 'make a difference', as noted earlier, was promoted by using the questionnaire results as a focus for discussion and problem-solving between staff and users in the ward/group. Vigorous attempts were made to involve users and staff in the research process through administering and collecting the questionnaires, analysing the data, and preparing the written feedback.

Data analysis: implications for users as researchers

The impact of the degree of involvement in the research in terms of promoting empowerment was not addressed explicitly in the research design, but both qualitative and quantitative data obtained through the project support the involvement of users in research, not only because of philosophical or methodological considerations, but also because involvement in research can promote empowerment, as defined by the study group.

Figure 8.1 The empowerment process

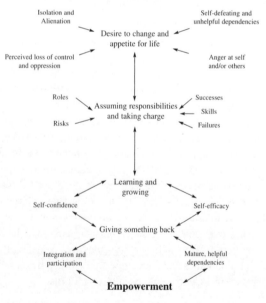

Figure 8.1 represents a model of the process of empowerment obtained from analysis of the quantitative data. An in-depth presentation and analysis of the data and discussion of the development of the model is not possible here, but it can be speculated that involvement in research activity could contribute to empowerment through the process detailed above.

Research can trigger or contribute towards a desire to change in a number of ways. An example of this is how reading research into user experiences and strategies, as in the Mental Health Foundation's 'Strategies for Living' project (Mental Health Foundation, 1997), can promote choice, control and consciousness-raising. Other recent research, such as the MIND study into experiences of stigma and discrimination (MIND 2000) and the Mental Health Foundation's survey of stigma (Mental Health Foundation, 2000), can also have a similar effect.

Although not measured in our project, direct involvement through providing data and participating in the discussions and feedback can also be a trigger for personal change and development by offering a broader perspective on experiences; survey informants in this research project were able to participate in genuine opportunities to reflect upon and contribute to the shaping of their environment. In some of the areas surveyed, the research experience provided one of very few opportunities available to broaden participants' perspectives and allow them to make a contribution. Thus, exposure to research studies and involvement as informants in user-defined research may help individuals to develop an appetite for life and fuel a desire to change their relationships with friends and family and the mental health system, and can promote a redefinition of self in relation to society through exposure to broader perspectives.

Empowerment, according to the study findings, involves developing personal responsibilities and reclaiming or adopting new roles, and exposing oneself to risk and the chance of achievement; with, of course, the possibility of setbacks from which to learn. Meaningful involvement in aspects of the research process can help here, from being part of the steering group, designing and piloting data collection tools, interviewing informants, analysing data, engaging in the change process, and writing up. Many user-focused projects now include training to prepare users as researchers, and there are training packs – for example, Mental Health Foundation (2001) – developed to help in the preparation. Involvement in a research project can provide not only opportunities for personal development but also a group context that can promote critical consciousness-raising and a commitment to mutual aid, which the study suggests is the most important context for empowerment.

An important aspect of becoming empowered, according to the people taking part in this study, involved a developing desire to help others. Mutual aid, either informally through peer groupings and support on the ward, or more formally through self-help or user-groups, was seen as a powerful forum for user empowerment. One important aspect of this experience was the realisation that people are uniquely able to help others through their own experiences, and that this in turn gives value to personal experiences and helps to redefine people away from being victims: the 'helper helped' or helper therapy principle (Riessman, 1965). This commitment to helping others is felt differently by different people; some get involved in user-involvement activity, some train as advocacy workers, and some participate in formal mutual-aid activity. Getting involved in research provides another forum where people can contribute to the welfare of others and 'give something back'.

The previous few paragraphs present a somewhat idealised picture, but I hope they illustrate how user involvement in research has potential as an important context for personal empowerment. The study also provided a wealth of quantitative data about the relationship between what happens in the ward/group and personal empowerment beliefs. The next few paragraphs will explore some of the statistical correlations[1] between items on the EEE and IEA questionnaires that support the usefulness of becoming involved in research to promote empowerment.

The importance of critical consciousness-raising to the empowerment process has already been acknowledged, and forms an important part of many authors' conceptions of empowerment (for example, Gibson, 1991; Minkler and Cox, 1980; Skelton, 1991; Campbell and Lindow, 1997). Five of the items on the EEE questionnaire formed a subscale that measured perceptions of how good the ward/group was in promoting critical consciousness-raising. These scores were then compared with scores for the subscales on the empowerment beliefs questionnaire (IEA) and the following significant correlations were noted. Positive perceptions of the environment regarding promoting consciousness-raising were correlated strongly to positive sense of self-worth ($p = 0.046$); trust in experts ($p = 0.005$); commitment to mutual aid ($p > = 0.0005$); and self-efficacy ($p = 0.005$). So, for this sample of 94 service users, critical consciousness-raising was related significantly to many empowerment outcomes.

In terms of individual items, positive perceptions in response to the statement 'this place helps me to understand the root causes of my problems' was correlated significantly to responses regarding 'feeling good about the way I am developing as a person' ($p = 0.002$); 'not feeling powerless most of the time' (p = 0.032); 'feeling I am often able to overcome barriers' (p = 0.040); trusting experts to make the right decisions about my health and welfare' (p = 0.018); 'feeling able to learn new things and skills' (p = 0.003;) and 'usually finding that being part of a group feels supportive' (p = 0.003). The potential for exposure to research studies and participation in research to promote critical consciousness-raising is evident, as is the significant relationship between consciousness-raising and other empowerment outcomes, including improved belief in individual personal power and self-efficacy.

Although the study did not address explicitly the impact of partnership and involvement in research on empowerment outcomes, it did study the impact of partnership in the care and treatment process through five items on the EEE questionnaire. Positive perceptions on this subscale[2] was correlated significantly to an improved sense of self-worth (p = 0.026). In terms of the individual items, statements about information and involvement in the care process yielded significant correlations with items measuring empowerment outcomes. Responses that signalled increasing satisfaction with the amount of information about the care and treatment someone was receiving was significantly positively correlated to the following beliefs:

- Confidence in expressing myself to people in authority (p = 0.042);
- Feeling good about the way I am developing as a person (p = 0.005);
- Believing that people have more power if they join together as a group (p = 0.014);
- Not feeling powerless most of the time (p = 0.001);
- Not thinking that professionals should listen to their clients more (p = 0.002);
- Not feeling I have very few options open to me regarding my future (p = 0.021);
- Not thinking that making waves never gets you anywhere (p = 0.007);
- Finding being in a group feels supportive (p = 0.014);
- Feeling more able to have fun these days (p = 0.021); and
- Having greater trust in experts to make the right decisions about my health and welfare (p = 0.002).

The positive effect on empowerment outcomes that results from satisfaction with information about care and treatment suggests the importance of training and ongoing collaboration and dialogue within research project teams, if user research is to promote empowerment in its participants. Users who, for example, train for a limited role as interviewers and do not have adequate information about the research as a whole may not find the experience so useful or valuable. This assertion is supported when examining the relationship between positive responses on another item that assesses perceptions of partnership and outcomes. Positive responses to the statement 'I feel fully involved in discussions about the care and treatment I am receiving show statistically significant positive correlations with the following empowerment beliefs:

- Feeling good about the way I am developing as a person ($p = 0.024$);
- Not feeling that getting angry about something never helps ($p = 0.002$);
- Not feeling that I have very few options open to me about my future ($p = 0.011$);
- Finding that being in a group feels supportive ($p = 0.049$); and
- Having greater trust in experts to make the right decisions about my health and welfare ($p = 0.019$).

Campbell and Lindow's (1997) call for mental health nurses to promote empowerment through the provision of information and partnership working is supported strongly by this data, with positive perceptions and satisfaction being associated significantly with improved self-esteem, more positive outlook, greater commitment to mutual aid and, crucially for professionals, greater trust in the role and judgement of experts through being a 'well informed patient' (Matzat, 1993).

This section has explored some of the implications of the data obtained in the research concerning the value and process of user-led research, and users as researchers. The qualitative data suggests that the reading of, and involvement in, research, may both fuel a desire for empowerment and provide a consciousness-raising context where empowerment is promoted. The quantitative data illustrates the importance of information and partnership in promoting empowerment in care settings, and suggests, by implication, that if these principles are embedded in the research process, the empowering potential of user research can be considerable.

Promoting partnership in research:
some lessons from the 'empowerment' project

In terms of promoting partnership and change, the project has had some success. One area improved its membership communication systems, and another instituted a community group as a result of the survey and feedback discussions. In one area, the second survey and feedback uncovered serious problems in terms of morale and practice, leading to ward discussions, managerial involvement, and the provision of an 'away day' for staff. Two of the five areas are to continue use of the questionnaires as part of their routine user involvement and clinical governance work. Some users offered and maintained a long-term involvement and commitment, with one helping to present the project to an audience of professionals within the area. A user-involvement week in the area was held as part of the project, with displays and talks from a variety of people promoting user-involvement and advocacy. Despite the successes, promoting involvement, partnership and change through the research has not been easy, and the impact could have been greater.

An important consideration in promoting partnership in a complex piece of research relates to where the individual sits in relation to influence and control of the project. Box 8.2 shows a diagram of the relationship of different groups to the research process.

Figure 8.2 Research control

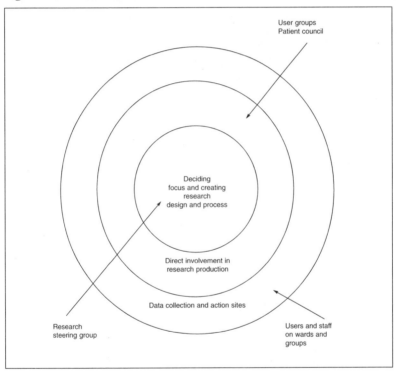

In broad terms, commitment to the research varied according proximity to the hub of the enterprise. The steering group was highly motivated, and the user groups and patients council members were very involved through the interviews and piloting of research tools. When it came to promoting involvement in the surveys in the wards and groups, however, commitment varied. Users in one ward in particular, seemed to resent the imposition of the survey and the implicit challenge to their milieu and practices; they did not appear to be in concordance with the research aims and philosophy. When working with users some distance from the locus of decision-making, who have had little input into shaping the process, finding appropriate ways of providing information and promoting involvement in the project is vital to the process.

Most survivor-led or focused research is inherently challenging. The early stages of this research were concerned with capturing the user experiences of those who had been cared for within the locality, these experiences being translated into the survey instruments. The administration of the questionnaires assessed the performance of staff and the organisation of ward or group against user-defined values and criteria, many of which were not shared by the professional and paid helpers responsible for providing care. Researchers promoting user values often find themselves working in an atmosphere of suspicion and conflict, with little support at times from users or staff. Serious consideration needs to be given to how appropriate emotional support is provided to any researchers performing what is often a lonely, stressful and frustrating job.

Careful thought needs to be given to cultivating relationships with gatekeepers. The original manager in the steering group was very keen and committed to the project and provided a real force for progress but, as is often the case, key players move on. As the research was undertaken on a part-time basis over six years (as is usual for part-time Ph.D. students), the research has seen several managers move on, and all the highly committed early members of the steering group have left the area. Careful thought needs to be given to the time-frame of such projects, to maximise consistency and to benefit from the energy and motivation that abounds early on. Such projects would also benefit from a half-time or full-time project leader, not someone like myself who has completed this on top of full-time working commitments. Some of the gatekeepers on the wards were, despite best efforts, indifferent, or even obstructive, to the survey process, whereas others used the opportunity of the research to promote participation and skills development in their clients.

The user-friendliness of the data collection tools needs to be assessed carefully in order to maintain interest and maximise response. The questionnaire packs that were administered to users were very long. The original EEE questionnaire had 54 items, and the IEA 36 items, plus demographic data, consent form and research information sheet.[3] Given this, the response rate of 54 per cent was very good and a testament to the staff, students and users/members who organised and undertook the administration of the questionnaires. There is clearly a trade-off between the amount and complexity of useful data that can be collected, and the involvement and participation of users in the research. Research whose primary aim is to empower its participants may have to consider accepting reduced data sets from participants.

Another barrier to commitment in the feedback and change process can occur through the way research data is presented. Theoretical formulations and presentation of qualitative data can be lengthy documents that just invite deposition in the wastebasket. The responses I received after returning transcripts for checking and analysis for comment were few; perhaps looking at these in the context of a face-to-face meeting would have worked better.

The problem of presenting quantitative data to users and staff is even more challenging, and after ten surveys, I have only recently arrived at a useful format. The first attempts involved lots of bar charts, tables, graphs and the like, then I developed booklets with similar information, plus clip-art and digital photos of some of the personnel involved. Despite my best efforts, though, the continued blank faces and lack of interest disheartened me and those who helped me. The way the data was being presented hindered, rather than encouraged, involvement. I now present very little quantitative data, concentrating mainly on key significant differences and relationships, and paying more attention to developing trigger questions to stimulate discussion and exploration.

A final issue relates to the way research can be affected by reliance on user representatives, and may become compromised by politics and hidden agendas. Two of the key early drivers and supporters of the research were advocates who were developing advocacy and user involvement in the locality. During the course of the research, support to one of the workers and his organisation was withdrawn and the service was closed, to be replaced a year or so later by a new organisation commissioned by the local user group and Health Authority. Sometime later, the other key player and supporter lost his job. Efforts were made to involve the new service in the project as the survey provided an ideal forum for new advocates to develop relationships and to promote the service, but the new organisation preferred not to get involved. This decision has no doubt lessened the impact of the research in promoting change and partnership. It appears that the research was seen as being associated with the previous organisation and personnel, so little active support was proffered. It is difficult to see how this could have been avoided, though if a broader base of user support for the project had been developed early on, with less reliance on the advocacy organisations, the research might have been better able to withstand the upheaval. On a personal note, I have worked very closely with the individuals involved, and got to know them very well. From mutual disclosure and partnership, friendships develop, and as a human being, I have been alongside them during some very distressing periods in their professional lives.

Conclusion

The social relations of the research I describe must seem very different from the positivistic notions of clinical research, where the researcher in someway captures the data without being affected personally or having any effect on the study site. This notion, even in 'scientific' or 'hard' research, is often heavily critiqued (see the Foreword in Rowan and Reason, 1990). In research like this, which aims to promote user involvement and empower participants, the positivistic notion of a value-free science and research process is shown to be almost absurd. While always aiming to maximise validity, reliability and rigour, the experience from this project is that research is, and ought to be, based on a set of beliefs and values. Research that aims to challenge, critique or change the existing order can only do so through social activity. The researcher who engages in this process can expect to feel excited, bored, frustrated, energised, powerless, exhilarated, depressed, deskilled and achieve a sense of personal satisfaction, and often all of these in a short space of time.

Notes

1. All correlations were calculated using the Pearson correlation technique. All probabilities are two-tailed. The sample size for the data presented ranges from 86 to 94.
2. The items on each questionnaire were placed into subscales measuring particular aspects. The subscales on the EEE questionnaire are 'Enabling staff qualities', 'Learning community', 'Strengths development', 'Safety', 'Consciousness-raising', 'Partnership', 'Needs focused care', and 'Commitment to mutual aid'. The subscales on the IEA questionnaire are 'Self-Worth', 'Trust in Experts', 'Desire for community involvement', 'Commitment to mutual aid' and 'Self-efficacy'. All subscales scored in excess of 0.7 in alpha reliability testing.
3. Anyone wishing to look at or use the questionnaires can obtain them from :
   Dr Tim Schafer, Anglia Polytechnic University, Ashby House, Brouk Street, Chelmsford, CM1 1SQ

References

Altheide, D L (1987) 'Ethnographic content analysis' *Qualitative Sociology*, 10 (1), Spring, pp 65–77

Campbell P and Lindow V (1997) *Changing Practice: Mental health nursing and user empowerment* MIND and RCN

Chesler, M A (1991) 'Participatory action research with self-help groups: an alternative paradigm for inquiry and action' *American Journal of Community Psychology* 19 (5), pp 757–68

Gibson, C H (1991) 'A concept analysis of empowerment' *Journal of Advanced Nursing* 16 pp 354–61

Heron, J (1996) *Co-operative Inquiry: Research into the human condition* London, Sage

Heron, J (1981) 'Philosophical basis for a new paradigm' in Reason, J and Rowan, J (eds) *Human Inquiry. A Sourcebook of New Paradigm Research* Chichester, Wiley

Matzat, J (1993) 'Away with the experts? Self-help groupwork in Germany' *Groupwork* 6 (1) pp 30–42

Mental Health Foundation (1997) 'Knowing our own minds: A survey of how people in emotional distress take control of their own lives' London, Mental Health Foundation

Mental Health Foundation (2000) 'Pull Yourself Together: A survey of people's experiences of stigma and discrimination as a result of mental distress' Press release, London www.mentalhealth org uk/pullyourselfsum htm

Mental Health Foundation (2001) *The DIY Guide to Survivor Research: Everything you always wanted to know about survivor led research but were afraid to ask* London, Mental Health Foundation

MIND (2000) *Counting the Cost* National Association for Mental Health

Minkler M and Cox K (1980) 'Creating critical consciousness in health: applications of Freire's philosophy and methods to the health care setting' *International Journal of Health Services* 10 (2) pp 311–22

Riessman, F (1965) 'The helper therapy principle' *Social Work* 10 (2) pp 27–32

Reason J and Rowan J (eds) (1981) *Human Inquiry. A Sourcebook of New Paradigm Research* Chichester, Wiley

Skelton, R (1994) 'Nursing and Empowerment: concepts and strategies' *Journal of Advanced Nursing* 19 pp 415–23

Taylor, M, Hoyes, L, Lart, R, and Means, R, (1992) *User Empowerment and Community Care: Unravelling the issues*, Studies in Decentralisation and Quasi-markets No 11, SAUS Publications, Bristol

Tesch, R, (1990) *Qualitative Research: Analysis Types And Software Tools* New York, Falmer

Wallcraft, J (1994) 'Empowering empowerment: professions and self-advocacy projects' *Mental Health Nursing* 14 (2) pp 6–9

Ward, D, and Mullender, A (1992) 'Empowerment and oppression: An indissoluble pairing for contemporary social work' *Critical Social Policy* 12 (2) pp 21–30

CHAPTER 9
Co-operative Inquiry in Cambridge and Sarajevo: Towards a Critical Understanding of Social Work Education

Reima Ana Maglajlic[1]

The reasons I initiated the research project outlined in this chapter are best summed up by the following two statements:

[In my education] *I learned to understand how policies worked, but not to make sense of them as part of a world I experienced. Nor did I find out much about what these policies might mean to the people for whose benefit they were intended* (Williams, 1993, p.3); and

For a science of persons as agents, my considered view of your reality without consulting you is a very different matter from our considered view of our reality. (Heron, 1981, p.27)

I set out to explore social work education with social work students, practitioners and service users, through a co-operative inquiry. There are examples of research that explored various facets of social work students' educational experiences (for example, Collins *et al.,* 1992; Aymer and Bryan, 1996; Gould and Harris, 1996; Jack and Mosley, 1997; Fernandez, 1998); social workers' attitudes towards their educational experience (for example, Gibbs and Cigno, 1986; Hindmarsh, 1992); their involvement in practice teaching (for example, Bell and Webb, 1992; Collins *et al.*, 1992); or their experiences of employment as social workers (for example, Borsay, 1989; Balloch, 1996; LaValle and Lyons, 1996a, 1996b); as well as service users' experiences in, and attitudes towards, social care (for example, Sathyamoorthy *et al.*, 1997; Mulhall, 2000).

There are also growing examples of service users acting as researchers (see, for example, Ford and Rose, 1997; McClelland, 1998; Evans and Fisher, 1999; Rose, 1999; Ramon, 2000; Humphries, 2001), and of frameworks and theory generated by users, based on their direct experiences of health and social care (Beresford, 2000). However, I found that previously these three groups, whose lives are affected in various ways by both social work education and practice, were not enabled to explore and influence these practices *together*, either through research or through practice initiatives. Readers might ask why these three stakeholder groups in social work education and practice be enabled to research together? Reinharz (1981) offers a reason:

> *Researchers, like social workers, live off the social problems they are*
> *supposed to ameliorate if there are no mechanisms making them*
> *accountable to those with 'the problem', and if their working conditions*
> *force them to perpetuate the problem rather than develop commitment*
> *to its resolution.'*

In a sense, I wanted to create an environment like this, which would enable students, practitioners and service users to share their expertise in joint exploration of social work education, particularly since they are rarely asked to do that together in order to research, plan or provide social and health care services.

Inviting involvement through a co-operative inquiry

In order to initiate such a study, I opted for an approach that 'married' co-operative inquiry and participatory action research (PAR) approaches:

> *The PAR strategy of developing knowledge through empowering dialogue*
> *initially between an animator and a community of people appears to be*
> *most appropriate when the inquiry involves a relatively large number of*
> *people who are initially disempowered. PAR also draws our attention to*
> *the political issues concerning ownership of knowledge, and to the need to*
> *create communities of people who are capable of continuing the PAR*
> *process ... Co-operative inquiry is a strategy more likely to be successful*
> *with a group of people who experience themselves as relatively empowered*
> *and who wish to explore and develop their practice together.* (Reason,
> 1994b, p. 335)

My aim was to initiate a group whose work would fall squarely between these two approaches. This can also be considered a counterpartal role inquiry (Heron, 1996), since the co-inquirers have different power and roles in the practice they are exploring. Participatory action research was selected because all the named stakeholder groups are still mainly disadvantaged in terms of active participation in the creation of policies and practices, in both education and social care. I wanted the groups to explore:

- What education ought to do;
- How education might do what it ought to do; and
- Which of their aims, strategies or behaviours educational practitioners
  would need to reform in order to educate more successfully (Torbert,
  1981), and would require exploration of political issues as noted
  above, as well as others (for example, economic policy).

I initiated two such groups, one at the Anglia Polytechnic University, Cambridge (UK) and one at the Department of Social Work, Faculty of Political Sciences, University of Sarajevo, Sarajevo, Bosnia and

Hercegovina. The first group worked together over five meetings for five months at the beginning of 1999, and the second worked together over five meetings for two months at the beginning of 2001.

In describing the initiation of the research, the work of the two groups and the research findings, I shall focus more on the role that users played in the work of these two groups, although this spotlight is placed artificially on this stakeholder group. With some issues and processes it is very hard to separate their involvement from that of other group members. However, attention to requirements for meaningful involvement was necessary, not just for group members who were service users, but also for each stakeholder group representatives.

At a minimum, for a research strategy to claim the term co-operative inquiry, I would argue that the nature of the involvement of all participants should be openly negotiated, that all should contribute to the creative thinking that is part of the research, and that relationships should aim to be authentically collaborative. (Reason, 1988, p. 9)

These dimensions may be difficult to satisfy because of the myriad ways in which 'open negotiation', 'contribution to creative thinking' and 'authentic collaboration' may be defined.

When initiating the group, I opted to contact local self-help groups, self-advocacy groups, support groups, and user-led and user-run projects to invite user co-inquirers, since I thought that the representatives of such groups would have experience of taking part in a variety of forums as well as in various forms of contact with professionals – from co-operation to lobbying, and hence be more likely to contribute as equally as possible to the sessions.

In Cambridge, there was no concise list of user initiatives 'across disabilities' – as professionals sometimes refer to the variety of people who at times become our service users – or across interests. Hence, I used the snowballing technique to access variety of groups. The Community Development Office held the most comprehensive list, and fifteen groups of various kinds were contacted over a period of three months. Six people decided to join my group:

- A member of a self-advocacy project for people with learning difficulties;
- A trustee for MENCAP who has learning difficulties;
- Three members of the local user-run mental health project; and
- A representative of the local Black Women's Support Group.

I asked a group member from the local user-run mental health project to be my co-facilitator, since we had already worked together on a year-long co-operative inquiry that helped the members in that project to evaluate their service.

Additional support was offered to service users to facilitate their equal and meaningful involvement – I reimbursed fares or organised transport for them, information shared with the group was available in writing (including large print), on tape, or through one-to-one meetings. Only one service user with learning difficulties asked for additional support.[2]

In Sarajevo, as when initiating the Cambridge group, I decided to contact the existing user associations that are active in Sarajevo canton (twelve in total). Out of the twelve associations, four representatives from three organisations offered to take part (president of the association of citizens with cerebral palsy, two executive committee members from 'Vita' (association of mental health service users in Sarajevo), and the president of the union of the civilian victims of war in Sarajevo canton).

The majority of service users who were members of the groups in Sarajevo and Cambridge suggested possible other members from among the social workers they knew. Suggestions were based on their experience of working with these social workers, and an introduction to the general topic of co-operative inquiry (social work education). Three of the suggested social workers in Sarajevo later became group members.

In Cambridge, 20 people in total joined the group – six people who use or have used social care services, nine students and five practitioners. These are the roles under which people were invited to join the group; some of us also had several others relevant to social work – as carers, practice teachers and students, as well as users and/or workers. Nearly half of the group members were men (nine), but the majority were women (eleven). Only one practitioner was male.

In Sarajevo, the group had fifteen members – six students (one first-year student, two third-year students, one fourth-year part-time student, one fourth-year full-time student, and one unemployed postgraduate student), five professionals (two working in the voluntary sector, one working in the health sector, one working in the local social services office, and one unemployed social worker), and four service users. There were four men in the Sarajevo group. While all the students were female, only one of the group of four service users was and only one practitioner was male. As with the Cambridge group, some participants had more than one stakeholder group status — some were both students and practitioners, while some were both users and students/practitioners.

Individual interviews and meetings

In initiating both groups, an interview was carried out with all interested potential participants. A brief interview guide was used, covering the following topics:

- What made you become a social worker/how did you first come in contact with social work?
- What are the experiences so far that shaped your opinion of social work learning and/or practice – both positive and negative?
- What made you become interested in joining the co-operative inquiry group?
- What do you expect to gain through your participation?

Afterwards, each person was sent:

- The notes from the interview to amend as required;
- A 'Layperson's guide to co-operative inquiry' by Peter Reason and John Heron, downloaded from the Centre for Action Research in Professional Practice website[3], and
- (for the Sarajevo group) A summary of the work from the Cambridge co-operative inquiry group.

The purpose of these preparation activities was to establish some area of a 'common ground' to initiate joint research on such a wide topic as social work education. Each of the participants was informed about the purpose of our individual meetings, and gave permission for 'individual data' to be used to this extent. A list of topics of joint interest emerged from the interviews was used in the initial meetings to help us to form a joint aim and framework for our work.

Group work
Cambridge
People wanted to join the group for a variety of reasons:

- For social workers, 'it could help me do my job better';
- For people who use services, 'it may help me to understand what social workers do';
- As students, 'it could help me to understand and do research better';
- 'It may help me see what works and what doesn't work in social work practice'; and
- 'It's good to be involved in something new'.

The group decided to focus its joint work on enquiry within the group (Heron, 1996). The group never split into smaller subgroups – one group member said 'We'd always be curious what the others were talking about.' The aim the group broadly set was to explore possible improvements to the current social work courses at the Anglia Polytechnic University (APU). However, this aim was modified over the five meetings.

The group drew on the following 'tools' to help make sense of its work:

- Personal experiences of social work education and practice (concrete examples);
- A summary of the Student Handbook for Diploma in Social Work students at the APU;
- A summary of research on social work education on following topics:
  - Why people choose to become social workers;
  - Becoming and being a social worker – private and professional identity;
  - Social work values, knowledge and skills;
  - Nature of social work practice;
  - Role of practice placements in social work education; and
  - Relationships with people who use social care services.

The summary included

- Sixty references to research undertaken since the mid-1970s;
- Diaries kept by group members; and
- A3-size summaries of various issues discussed in previous meetings.

Through its exploration, the group finally concluded its work by identifying a few 'ingredients'/skills found to be lacking in, yet relevant to, social work learning and practice. The findings of the group's work were written up by the co-facilitator and myself, and reviewed by the group. A version of this report was shared and discussed with the staff at the APU.

The majority of service users, apart from the co-facilitator, atended only between one and three meetings. The most common excuse for non-attendancee was lack of time, and other commitments. One service user confessed that she found it hard to follow the meetings and contribute to them. Also, her motivation to join the group didn't stem from an interest in the topic, or a desire to be involved in a research project. She told me that the main reason she wanted to join the group was because she felt isolated and wished to make friends. We discussed this in a sense that – as in any other life situation – she may or may not find friends through the group. We also explored what interests she might have regarding the topic. She was determined to join, but attended only three meetings.

Sarajevo

All the participants said that the central topic of interest was the impact of the social and economic situation on social work practice in BiH. However, a theme emerged – 'what can we do as a group?' – that offered this group a more proactive role and combined a co-operative inquiry structure with that

of participatory action research (PAR) (Fals-Borda and Rahman, 1991) -
This role for the group was initiated by the service-user member:

> *We can't talk about this work, without talking about the politics,*
> *because all is politics. This is unfortunately our reality. What can we*
> *as a group do about the impact of the social and economic situation on*
> *social work practice? ... How powerful are we? We can express our*
> *opinions, but it's government and its institutions that should do*
> *something about it. That is the core of our problems – both for social*
> *workers and for the users.*

This duality – both that the group has an obligation to do something to
change the status quo, and its the fear that it would be unable to achieve this,
remained with us as a guiding theme for the rest of the meetings.

Apart from the impact of the socioeconomic factors on social work practice
in BiH, the group chose as the aim of their work to find a sustainable way to
enable co-operation between the department of social work and practice insti-
tutions and user organisations, considering the current socioeconomic situation
in Bosnia and Hercegovina. To address this aim, the group drew on:

● Personal experiences of social work education and practice (concrete
  examples);

● A review of the curriculum of the social work programmes in
  Sarajevo, as well as in Croatia, Slovenia, and an example of a UK
  programme (APU);

● A summary of research on social work education (see above);

● Notes from previous meetings; and

● The findings from a survey among social work students and practitioners
  in Sarajevo, conducted by the group members, based on a questionnaire
  composed by the group members.

At the end of the group work, the findings were presented and discussed with
the head of the Department of Social Work at APU and presented subsequently at the departmental meeting.

Both groups aimed to move through cycles of reflection and action, with
the Sarajevo group being more successful in meeting the latter objective.
This group had more contacts with their peers outside the group, used the
opinions and experiences of these peers in the group's work, and exchanged
ideas with them. I believe this helped them to move away from the focus on
within-group reflection, much more a feature of the work of the Cambridge
group.

Findings

In both groups, service-user members were the main initiators of the discussions concerning the aims of the work of both groups, as well as in defining the findings in both groups. In parallel, they all had fears that they would not be vocal enough, or skilled enough, to take part. These fears were proven to be unfounded.

The work of both groups complemented the other well: for example, an 'answer' to the question posed at the beginning of the work of the Sarajevo group was formulated by the members of the Cambridge group. While discussing the emphasis on competence in British social work education, they emphasized the relevance of taking responsibility for one's own practice, for action taken or not made (particularly with reference to criticisms of inaction that may have enabled the maintenance of the status quo).

Both groups made several recommendations for social work courses pertaining to more active user involvement in social work education:

- Service users and practitioners should be encouraged, supported and paid to co-teach on social work courses. In some parts of Britain, there are 'Users as Teachers' groups (for example, in Portsmouth). Involvement should be ongoing; one-off visits do not enable discussion and learning. Users should also be involved in course management, student admission procedures and student assessments.

- Forums such as the ones initiated for the purpose of this study (with various social work stakeholder groups working together) are beneficial both for active service user and practitioner involvement in the course and for a more critical understanding of social work practice by students. These multi-partner forums should not be separated from the course, but be an integral part of it, involved in making a variety of decisions that shape the social work course in question as well as enabling students to discuss issues raised in various modules with their peers in practice and service users.

More user-led initiatives in social care would support and ease such developments. Their importance is in the following: users with experience of participation in such projects are more likely to state their views more openly when among professional 'strangers'. They are used to challenging professionals more freely, and would be able to support and be role models for other participating users. User involvement is a term often discussed but rarely understood. Many projects carry this title, but below the surface, either professionals or 'professionalised' users are pulling strings of 'participation' of others, who primarily obey and follow.

These issues need to be addressed in future developments with similar groups. On the whole, the groups' development supports one of the groups' findings, namely that it was through the value of our ongoing mutual relationships (particularly with myself as the group initiator and facilitator) that people felt able to participate:

"People at L. know you" You have to take that into account. You have been seen there, since you were doing other things with them. And therefore we felt confident to come and join the group (Service user).

Once in the group, members were drawn to its focus (experiences of social work education and practice) and format:

It is interesting to find out about what social workers do and don't do, and how they think and feel about it. It is enabling to find out that even social workers feel at loss at times, and explore what we can do together
(Service user).

In Cambridge, however, some people found it hard to cope; few found the experience irrelevant, and left. For people who use services, a payment for participation may help them to overcome initial anxieties about working with professionals and students.

Conclusion

The co-facilitator's diary in Cambridge pinpointed some of my concerns about the groups' aims and decisions:

*Our group seems to have promoted the notion of partnership rather than patronisation, but this seems to me to run into the problem of **whose interests exactly does this profession represent**. It glosses over the difficult mediating role which social workers often have to play.*

I think another factor behind the negative public image of social workers is that they are always likely to fall foul of one party or the other because they have loyalties to several. And perhaps this lies behind some of the disillusionment felt by the students. One person I spoke to has considered a social work course with the view of fighting the corner of the oppressed (forming partnerships with needy clients) but reckoned that nowadays he would simply be drawn into the role of 'soft policing'...(Service user's diary)

My concern is that the Cambridge group did not take responsibility for the issues they identified as being important. They also saw the possible continuation of a group such as ours as an opportunity to 'step away' from their everyday practice, rather than as an opportunity to plan and influence their own practice in a different way. It was, at best, seen as a useful supervision tool.

These concerns are not just a result of the wish to influence or initiate change. One of the surprises of my previous experiences of facilitating action research such as this one was that it helped the group to identify what needed preserving, not just what needed altering in the future development of the organisation we evaluated through a co-operative inquiry. [4]

Although the research group concluded that taking responsibility for one's own practice is important in both social work education and practice, they were united in shying away from implementing their own conclusions. This is not an easy or brief process. It was considered that, ultimately, it would be the facilitator's responsibility to do something with the study results. Partly, I believe, it is also because of what people usually associate with participation in research – the process, as well as the results, usually 'belongs' to someone else; I was asked by a few members during our six months' work, 'Are we achieving what you want us to?'

The Sarajevo group had a different ending. Students took on the responsibility of implementing the group findings and planned to work with other group members in the following academic year to develop a series of lectures to be given by both social workers and service users at the Department.

After these experiences, I believe that we still have a lot to learn, preserve, recall and change in order to develop reciprocity and mutuality in working with the people who use services, through a variety of research and practice initiatives:

> *Many people know about the ideas we have reviewed here, but a few know them deeply and fewer practice them. We need to learn how to make these ideas part of our experiential and practical knowledge, so that they can be applied during the stickiest moments of our inquiry, not just stuck up on the wall to be admired* (Rowan, 1981; p. 137).

Notes

1. Project manager, Tempus Phare Project 'Community Mental Health', BiH, rea@bih.net.ba
2. She sat next to me in the meetings and nudged me when she wanted to speak, since she found it hard to get her word in at the pace discussions developed at times. We also met a few times to discuss the notes and her comments. I was asked to present her views at the following meeting.
3. http://www.bath.ac.uk/management/carpp/layguide.htm
4. This was a co-operative evaluation with the representatives of a Cambridge-based user-run mental health organisation.

References

Aymer, C and Bryan, A (1996) 'Black students' experience on social work courses: accentuating the positives', *British Journal of Social Work*, 26, pp 1–16

Balloch, S (1996) 'Experiences of training in the statutory social services', in Connelly, N (ed.) *Training Social Services Staff: Evidence from new research Research* in Social Work Education No 4, NISW, London, pp 9–17

Bell, L and Webb, SA (1992) 'The invisible art of teaching for practice; Social workers' perceptions of taking students on placement', *Social Work Education*, 11(1), pp 28–46

Beresford, P (2000) 'Service users' knowledge and social work theory: conflict or collaboration' *British Journal of Social Work*, 30, pp 489–503

Borsay, A (1989) 'First child care, second mental health, third the elderly: Professional education and the development of social work priorities' *Research Policy and Planning*, 7, pp 22–30

Collins, S, Ottley, G and Macmurran, M (1992) 'Student and practice teacher perceptions of the enabling role in practice teaching' *Social Work Education*, 11(2), pp 20–40

Evans, C and Fisher, M (1999) 'Collaborative evaluation with service users: moving towards user-controlled research' in Shaw, I and Lishman, J (eds) *Evaluation and Social Work Practice*, London, Sage

Fernandez, E (1998) 'Student perceptions of satisfaction with practicum learning' *Social Work Education*, 17(2), pp 173–201

Ford, R and Rose, D (1997) 'Heads and tales' *Health Service Journal*, 6 November, pp 28–9

Gibbs, I and Cigno, K (1986) 'Reflections from the field: the experience of former CSS and CQSW students' *British Journal of Social Work*, 16(3), pp 289–309

Gould, N and Harris, A (1996) 'Student imagery of practice in social work and teacher education: a comparative research approach' *British Journal of Social Work,* 26, pp 223–37

Heron, J (1981) 'Philosophical basis for a new paradigm', in Reason, P and Rowan, J (eds) (1981) *Human Inquiry: A sourcebook of new paradigm research* Chichester, Wiley, pp 19–35

Heron, J (1996) *Co-operative Inquiry: Research into the human condition* London, Sage

Hindmarsh, J H (1992) 'The impact of a university qualifying course: new graduates' accounts' *Issues in Social Work Education*, 12, pp 2–23

Humphries, B (2001) 'Putting participative research into practice' *Care Plan*, March, pp 23–5

Jack, R and Mosley, S (1997) 'The client group preferences of diploma in social work students: What are they, do they change during programmes and what variables affect them' *British Journal of Social Work*, 27, pp 893–911

La Valle, I and Lyons, K (1996a) 'The social worker speaks: I – perceptions of recent changes in British social work' *Practice*, 8(2), pp 5–14

La Valle, I and Lyons, K (1996b) 'The social worker speaks: II – management of change in the personal social services' *Practice*, 8(3), pp 63–71

McClelland, F (1998) 'Monitoring our services ourselves' *Mental Health Care* 1(8), pp 272–4

Mulhall, J (2000) 'Using Community Mental Health Services: asking users' *Practice*, 12(4), pp 27–36

Ramon, S (2000) 'Participative mental health research: users and professional researchers working together' *Mental Health Care*, 3(7), pp 224–8

Reason, P (1988) 'Introduction', in Reason, P (ed) *Human Inquiry in Action: developments in new paradigm research*, London, Sage, pp 1–17

Reason, P (1994a) 'Introduction', in Reason, P(ed.) *Participation in Human Inquiry* London, Sage, pp 1–6

Reason, P (1994b) 'Three approaches to participative inquiry', in Denzin, N K and Lincoln, Y S (eds) *Handbook of Qualitative Research* London, Sage pp 324–39

Rose, D (1999) 'Do it yourselves' *Mental HealthCare*, 2(5), pp 174–7

Rowan, J (1981) 'A dialectical Paradigm for Research', in Reason, P and Rowan, J (eds) op cit, pp 93–112

Sathyamoorthy, G, Ford, R and Warner, L (1997) 'Telling tales' *Community Care*, 14–20 August, pp 32–3

Torbert, W R (1981a) 'Why educational research has been so uneducational: the case for a new model of social science based on collaborative inquiry', in Reason, P and Rowan, J (eds) op cit, p 141–51

Williams, F (1993) 'Thinking – exploring the 'I' in ideas', in Shakespeare, P, Atkinson, D and French, S (eds) *Reflecting on Research Practice: Issues in health and social welfare* Buckingham, Open University Press, pp 11–24

CHAPTER 10
The Experience of the Transition from Psychiatric Hospital to Community: The First Consumer-Run Research Project in Israel

Avigdor Petrank and Israel J. Sykes

In the not too distant past the common social practice in most Western countries with regard to people with mental illness was to institutionalise them in state-run asylums or psychiatric hospitals. This practice reflected both society's fear of people with mental illness, who were thereby taken away from community life, but also the lack of hope regarding their potential for recovery. Hospitalisation was seen as the best available solution to meet the needs of both society for protection, and the mentally ill for maintenance care.

Since the early 1960s a number of factors have converged that have reversed this direction, in mental health as well as with regard to other populations with disabilities:

- A growing recognition of the harm inflicted by institutionalisation, and a subsequent push towards de-institutionalisation;
- Improvements in methods of treatment (for example, medications, models of rehabilitation) that make more independent life in the community a viable option;
- Increasingly outspoken consumer organisations that advocate more humane forms of treatment and the adoption of policies enabling people with disabilities to live with dignity; and
- Recognition that hospitalisation is a costly intervention, and that supports in the community may ultimately be cheaper for the taxpayer.

In Israel, as elsewhere, de-institutionalisation and the development of community supports have been on the mental health policy agenda since the early 1970s. Until recently, this agenda has been espoused but rarely carried out, with only slowly declining rates of hospitalisation, and with only minimal investment in community support.

In 2000 the Israeli parliament (the Knesset) passed a new law, according to which people with mental illness are entitled to rehabilitation services in the community, and the Ministry of Health is engaged in promoting a dual agenda, reducing hospitalisation rates while concurrently developing opportunities for housing, employment, leisure time and educational activities. This effort is an uphill battle, but under way none the less .

The present research study addresses an important but often overlooked facet of the transition from hospitalisation to the community, namely the

123

experience of individuals with mental illness who undergo the transition. What is this move like for them? What do they find helpful? What do they find obstructs their progress? How could services be better organised to assist them in this transition? This study builds on an emerging tradition, particularly in Britain, of research performed by mental health service users (Ramon and Tallis, 1997; Rose, 2000).

It is the first such study to be carried out in Israel. The use of service users as researchers is seen to have the following advantages:

- Users' knowledge and understanding of their own situation is an essential, and frequently missing, component within the field of mental health, which may challenge and/or corroborate professional understanding;

- User-researchers are more likely than other researchers to have street credibility among other users, more likely than others to identify the issues of concern to them, and are more likely to employ research methods with which they feel comfortable;

- Users can become researchers within a relatively short time if provided with training and payment; and

- The experience of working as researchers can be meaningful and empowering.

According to Ramon (2000), British experience has demonstrated the viability and added value of employing users as researchers. Given adequate training and support, users carried out good-quality interviews, with few problems. The users in both capacities (interviewer and interviewee) reported having enjoyed the experience. Furthermore, it was found that user-interviewers were able to obtain information from interviewees that users would have been unlikely to disclose to non-user-researchers. Finally, while some user-researchers suffered relapses during the research projects, they were none the less able to return to their roles and carry out their required tasks.

The present study
Participating organisations
The study in Israel was initiated by Professor Shula Ramon from Anglia Polytechnic University at Cambridge, and is being carried out collaboratively by representatives of the following organisations: Benafshenu – Bridges to Recovery, a project of the non-profit organisation Shekel (community services for the disabled) with users and relatives as members; the School of Social Work in Ben Gurion University, Beer Sheva; the Beer Sheva Mental Health Centre; and the Jerusalem Mental Health Centre (Kfar Shaul and Eitanim hospitals).

Developmental phases

Phase 1

In August 2000, a two-day training session was held in Jerusalem, facilitated by Max Lachman (Ministry of Health, researcher into recovery from an experiential, narrative, perspective); Shula Ramon (researcher, experienced in initiating user research); Vered Slonim-Nevo (family therapist, researcher of psychotherapy and immigration); and Israel Sykes (user leader, researcher into children and families), and attended by six users, four from Jerusalem recruited by Benafshenu (two study coordinators and two interviewers), and two (interviewers) from Beer Sheva recruited by professional staff at the Beer Sheva Mental Health Centre. The training provided an opportunity for participants to learn about the proposed study and about users acting as researchers, and to begin to learn and practice basic interviewing skills.

It was proposed at the time that 30 users (20 from Jerusalem, 10 from Beer Sheva) would be interviewed, at two points in time: (i) three months following release; and (ii) six months following release. It was hoped that through this series of interviews it would be possible to capture the process of transition to the community, and develop insights as to different needs at different stages. (At a later stage it was decided to add a further interview close to the time of release from hospitalisation.)

Phase 2

Following the training described above it became apparent that access to users moving to the community required active collaboration with psychiatric hospitals, and that this could only happen after the study had been approved by Helsinki Committees in both Jerusalem and Beer Sheva. This convention functions in a similar way to the UK ethics committees. First in Jerusalem, and then in Beer Sheva, psychiatrists who saw the value of the study, helped to put it on the agenda of the appropriate committees, frame it in ways that made it acceptable, and saw through its passage. This process was time-consuming (about six months), and frustrating, as it made it impossible to move ahead with interviews following the training. On the other hand, it advanced the credibility of the study and enhanced the partnerships with important functionaries in the participating psychiatric hospitals.

Phase 3: Initial implementation

Once Helsinki approval was obtained, the study co-ordinator from Benafshenu (Avigdor Petrank) (the other co-ordinator had meanwhile left the team, expecting her first child) faced the task of recruiting interviewees from among individuals hospitalised in the closed and open wards of Kfar Shaul, the Jerusalem hospital to which we had access initially. Avigdor therefore made contact with professionals in the hospital, including holding meetings with the directors of the wards and with the hospital social work staff, to tell them about the study and encourage them to inform the study staff about individuals who were soon to be released. Hospital staff responded with interest, but it was unclear at this early stage whether they would in fact take an active stance with regard to the study.

Phase 4: From crisis to opportunity
At around this time, Avigdor began to de-compensate, developing psychotic symptoms and refusing medication, a condition that ultimately led to his forced hospitalisation in the closed ward of Kfar Shaul – the same hospital from which he was recruiting interviewees. The initial fear was that, without him, the study would fall apart. After several weeks of hospitalisation (the success of which was enhanced by interventions with hospital staff by the psychiatrist with whom Avigdor had collaborated), he began to recover. By then he was able to begin to utilise his hospitalisation as an opportunity: both to learn about the hospital and hospitalisation as a participant–observer, and to make connections with fellow users who, already knowing him, agreed to participate in the study.

After his release, Avigdor returned to the hospital to hold meetings with staff and user groups. Initially, he encountered a certain amount of hesitation on the part of staff, who, having seen him during his crisis, questioned whether they felt comfortable allowing him access to their patients. This was in part because, for a period of about a month after release he was still not back to normal health, as an optimum combination of medications had still not been found. Once he was better stabilised, however, and with the help of the deputy director of the hospital, he was again better received by hospital staff.

Meanwhile, Avigdor was himself interviewed by other interviewers in Jerusalem, and several of the individuals whom he met while hospitalised were interviewed by him or by one of the other interviewers.

Phase 5: Initiating referrals
Following this initial wave of interviews, efforts focused on developing ways to gain access through professional gatekeepers in the Jerusalem and Beer Sheva hospitals. This experience has been less successful than was hoped, despite the interest and willingness to co-operate that professionals have demonstrated. When it came down to the level of concrete referrals, for some reason these were not forthcoming.

Initial findings

By this stage, eight individuals had been interviewed at least once. In the following section we shall put forward some of the insights gained from both the process of the study up to this point, and from an initial evaluation of the content of these preliminary interviews.

Findings that emerged in the process of the study

The ambiguity of the point of transition

When conceptualising the study initially, the phrase 'transition from the hospital to the community' seemed clear and unambiguous. In reality, in the course of meetings with professionals in both hospital and community settings, the boundaries between hospital and community became blurred. It is clear on the one hand that people in closed hospital wards are hospitalised, and that individuals living with their families or in supported housing with outpatient care are in the community; and indeed, some people are released directly to the community.

But what about partial hospitalisation, when people live at home but come daily to spend each morning at the hospital? Or rehabilitation wards, in which individuals live in the hospital but work outside the hospital every day? Thus we found that many people's transition to the community was through hospital-based programmes, and we needed to decide where to draw the line. In practice, especially in light of the difficulty in recruiting interviewees, we agreed to view these hospital-based programmes as being 'in the community' for the purposes of the study.

User/researcher/professional collaboration

One of the successes of the study, which can by no means be taken for granted, is a high level of collaboration between representatives from three different sectors: users; researchers; and mental health professionals. The idea for the study was put forward initially by a researcher from abroad, but it could only begin to move forward when it was embraced by a consumer-based project (Benafshenu). An important part of Benafshenu's ethos, promoted by the Benafshenu director (Israel Sykes), himself both a user and a professional, is the importance of working together with professionals in order to promote change. Indeed, Benafshenu staff have discovered repeatedly that, when approached with this attitude, professionals are often pleased about and responsive to consumer initiatives.

In the case of this study, a high degree of collaboration was necessary, both to gain acceptance in Helsinki Committees, and to gain access to potential interviewees. While in the first instance there was success, the second is still somewhat at an impasse and requires further work and understanding.

Difficulties in recruiting interviewees

Although ready to support the study in principle, very few referrals came directly from the professional staff. This raises the possibility that a number of professionals were more hesitant about a user-researcher's project than was overtly expressed. Was this due to fear of criticism that users might express more readily to a user-researcher than to a professional researcher? Would they have been equally reluctant in the case of *any* outsider interviewing 'their' patients?

As described earlier, the present study builds on experience in Britain with the use of user-researchers. On the basis of that experience, it was assumed that in Israel the use of user-researchers would also act to motivate potential interviewees to participate in the study; we have not found this to be the case, however. Users, on the whole, have been reluctant to take part. We have the following hypotheses about why:

- Some users want to put the hospitalisation behind them, and are reluctant to enter a conversation that might take them back there;
- Others are afraid to expose their illness to anyone, explanations about the study notwithstanding;
- Some have refused to take part because of the opposition of family members, for whom it is important that the fact of the illness is kept secret;
- Several people have asked the question, 'What's in it for me?' The suggestion that the study might contribute to improving services in the transition from hospital to the community has been unconvincing, as most of the users are still 'in the closet' and not interested in making such a contribution;
- Some users who agreed to participate two weeks before release found themselves unwell following release, and felt unable to speak in the interview; and
- In Beer Sheva on several occasions individuals indicated that they would participate in the study, but only on condition that interviewers were professionals and not users.

Difficulties in arranging interviews

Not all user-researchers in fact, arranged interviews as soon as they were given names and addresses of potential interviewees. This perhaps highlights a lack of self-confidence and lack of sufficient internal, ongoing, support within the group of user-researchers.

Willingness to speak openly to user interviewers

While there was some indication of a reluctance to agree to being interviewed by users, in several of the interviews it was possible to see that interviewees found it easier to discuss their experiences with people who were themselves users and who could identify with their experiences, sometimes to the point of saying things they would be unlikely to have said to a professional. One woman said, for example: 'I worked as a salesperson in a pharmacy chain and she [the doctor] came to see me and I didn't want to tell her where I was going, I was in a state, I don't really like to talk about it, you understand? You understand?'

Another person told about how he was transferred to an open ward after an extensive stay in a closed ward, and after less than twenty-four hours he refused to stay there. Staff gave him the choice of returning to the closed ward, if not willingly, then by force. He went on to say: 'People ask me if there was a specific reason, I don't know, I think I didn't like the atmosphere there, how the place looked. It could be that the reasons were emotional or confused, something connected to illogical things that I was still thinking at the time.' He did not share these thoughts with his therapists when he was returned to the closed ward, and it is likely that he would not have admitted to them if he had not known that the interviewer had had similar experiences.

Initial findings: content analysis of interviews

While it is obviously too early in the study to draw any conclusions, a number of interesting trends have become apparent.

Difficulties experienced in the closed ward

Interviewees who were hospitalised in the closed ward complained that their stay there was difficult. The sight of the other patients was hard to bear. Some noted that when they were in a psychotic state they did not care about the others, as they were immersed in their own experience. One was occupied with voices and visions. A second with anxieties. One of the interviewees noted: 'It's very hard for me the thing with drugs. I got sick and I didn't do that on purpose, but people who take drugs and are hospitalised, that really bothered me.'

Another interview noted that when he came out of his psychotic state it hurt him to see patients restricted and the difficult ways in which they were treated.

Passivity of users vis á vis the treatment professionals

One interesting characteristic of interviewees is that they were often unaware of options they had when leaving hospital, and have tended to accept unquestioningly the solutions offered to them by treatment staff. For example:

'Apparently they decided that my functioning is okay and I am fit to return to the community, to a regular environment, and the unit for supported housing prepares you for life in normal society'. This passivity was taken for granted by the Israeli team, and was therefore invisible to them. It became visible only when contrasted with the experiences presented in the British projects. While the consumer movement in Israel has made great strides since the mid-1990s, this finding sheds light on how much work is yet to be done in promoting user awareness of options and rights, and particularly in promoting a more proactive stance towards their recovery.

Frequency of delayed community placement and its costs

One complaint that has been repeated concerns the long wait for community-based housing and employment. Having recovered, with the aid of medication, from the psychosis that led to hospitalisation, they feel caught in a frustrating limbo between hospital and community. Making matters worse, while in this limbo state, they face many unfilled hours of boredom. While in the morning there is occupational therapy or work in the hospital laundry or warehouse, the rest of their day is empty. This freedom from responsibility is somewhat calming, but is also accompanied by anxiety as to how it will affect their ability to adapt to life on the outside.

The following statement was made by a man who moved from the closed ward directly to the 'supported housing' ward (in which people are prepared for the transition to supported housing), where he has lived for six months while waiting for housing and employment in the community: 'What the stay here gives is a break to think, to calm down ... On the other hand, I know that it will be difficult to leave and the longer I stay here the harder it will be for me to leave.' Some of the people released from the open ward become day patients. For some this is a transitional period until housing and employment solutions are found. One interviewee, while a day patient, found himself, without the assistance of hospital staff, both work in the private sector and independent housing. However, after six months he was re-hospitalised with depression.

In contrast, one woman who moved to her own home and became a day patient for six months, and was referred subsequently to an outpatient-based rehabilitation unit, said the following: 'Even when I left gradually from June to December I continued to go to E. [the psychiatric hospital] and afterwards to the project [the rehabilitation unit] which helped me ... The treatments that I receive, the music and art therapy, the regular therapy, helped me a lot.'

Conclusion

This study has been both rewarding and frustrating for those involved. It has been rewarding in the positive collaborations that have been built up and maintained between users, researchers and professionals, but has been frustrating in that progress, in terms of the numbers of interviews, has been much slower than envisioned. This has had a significant cost in that there has not been enough work to occupy the staff who embarked on the project with us, thus leaving them somewhat in limbo as to their role in the project.

When we were first approached to write this chapter, our reaction was that we have done so little of what we planned to do, and we have so little data, that we could not possibly have anything of value to write. However, the work of writing the chapter has brought to light what we hope are some valuable experiences and insights, both about the current state of affairs in Israel and about the cross-cultural application of user-performed research. To summarise these briefly here:

- Collaboration between users, professionals and researchers in Israel is not only possible, but is in certain circles welcomed, as a refreshing and promising breakthrough. However, covert reluctance may play a part;
- A vanguard of users in Israel are ready to take on the roles of user-researchers, and they need on-going support;
- Other users in Israel, more than elsewhere seem to experience difficulties in accepting this image change for service users. For those who do accept his role shift, however, the benefits reported elsewhere seem to hold true;
- Users in Israel seem to be characterised by a relatively passive stance *vis á vis* the 'system', and are burdened by stigma and the need to hide their illness; and
- The boundary between the hospital and the community is ambiguous. There is, on the one hand, an orientation towards community living, but in practice the lack of available services leaves many users within hospital-based programmes in limbo as they wait for placements.

Finally, our most significant learning is that this journey is unpredictable, and takes time and patience, and the ability to persevere. It is our hope that, over the year working on the project, we have laid the foundations for the fruition of this specific journey, and no less for many future research collaborations with users in Israel.

References

Oliver, M (1992) Changing the social relations of research production? *Disability, Handicap & Society*, 7 (2) pp 101–13

Ramon, S (2000) 'Participative mental health research: users and academics working together' *Mental Health Care* 3 (7) pp 224–8

Ramon, S Tallis D (1997) Seamless services and rebuilding identity: towards a different research agenda, *Breakthrough*

Rose, D (2001) *Users' Voices: The perspectives of mental health service users on community and hospital care* London, Sainsbury Centre of Mental Health

CHAPTER 11
Doing Research Together: The Forum for Collaboration with Users in Research (Folk.us) at Exeter University
Rachel Purtell, Lisa Baxter and Annie Mitchell

The idea for Folk.us was conceived in 1997 by a group of people committed to working in partnership, and to the empowerment and participation of people using public services. The emphasis on evidence-based practice and collaboration in health service and social care research seemed a productive channel for creating partnerships across those fields. Folk.us wanted to find out if collaborative research was realistic in an academic context. We wanted to know if service users, professionals and academics could really 'do research together'. Folk.us wanted to create a mutually supportive network that would facilitate the empowerment of service users, carers and lay people, both as individuals and collectively, using the creation of knowledge through research.

Evidence from community psychology (Orford, 1992), suggests that social support and social power make a positive difference to individual and community health and well-being. In Exeter, there is a community ethos in the local clinical psychology service. Some of these professionals were already working in partnership with service users and carers in training initiatives. This was a starting point for a research interest group that included service users and professionals. Folk.us has been fortunate in having key people who encouraged innovation in research and user involvement. Folk.us has its headquarters in the School of Psychology at University of Exeter because Annie Mitchell, its director and a Lecturer in Clinical and Community Psychology, developed this work as one of her research activities, though this is a less traditional approach to research.

Supporters of Folk.us include the local NHS Research and Development Support Unit; the local Centre for Evidence-Based Social Services; the Regional NHS Executive; and the national Consumers in NHS Research Support Unit. Sponsors include the School of Psychology at the University of Exeter; the North and East Devon Health Authority; Devon Social Services; the former Exeter and East Devon Community Health Care Trust; and the local department of Clinical and Community Psychology.

Our original aim was to build a network of service users, lay people and professionals from different agencies in North and East Devon, which would promote a research culture that is 'meaningfully controlled and/or influenced by service users and carers '. In March 1999, Folk.us held a conference in Exeter called 'Research: Who 's it for anyway? ' The conference included national speakers, and workshops presented by service users, carers and professionals. The conference attracted a wide audience of service users, lay people and professionals, and the event made a lasting impression on some of those who attended. These are some of the comments made:

[My] strongest memory is how much all these people had in common through mental health or physical health – I felt we weren 't alone. I found this out when I went round talking to users. There were so many experiences we shared. When I asked them questions and they started giving me their experiences, I agreed with all that they were saying.
(Service user)

[The speaker 's] ability to articulate the case for user-led services with simultaneous passion and clarity was as great in person as in print. I was left wondering how the issues could seem controversial at all.
(Mental health professional)

Following this conference, Folk.us, applied for and received funding from the NHS Executive South West Research and Development, to develop a programme to support user involvement in research in North and East Devon. A part-time co-ordinator was recruited to facilitate the empowerment and support of service users and carers in conducting and participating in research on their own terms. The first post holder, Sally Bourne, was succeeded by Rachel Purtell, who has both worked within and been an active member of the user movement.

Folk.us is especially proud of having strengthened links in research between health and social care services; inter-agency co-operation is difficult to achieve, as each agency is working to its own priorities and within its own financial constraints.

Folk.us's initial aims:
- To provide a forum in which users and carers can meet with professionals to discuss issues of common concern around research;
- To encourage applications to funding bodies that are planned jointly with those who use the services;
- To provide support to those who are endeavouring to do collaborative research;
- To encourage research partnerships between lay people/users and professionals;
- To promote mutual learning by the development of educational tools and training events;

- To think actively about how findings that are of particular concern to users can be fed back into practice;
- To network locally and further afield with those who are interested in collaborative research;
- To learn about the strengths and pitfalls of collaborative research, consider how difficulties need to be addressed, and find ways of addressing training needs; and
- To disseminate the outputs of Folk.us.

Developing Folk.us

Folk.us is no different from most projects that aim to develop a culture of user and carer involvement. We have faced challenges presented by both our work and limited resources in terms of staff time and funding. Health and social research are at the centre of our agenda but, as we know, research has been, and still is largely, the bastion of academics, scientists and professionals (Oliver, 1997). Folk.us is faced with a real challenge to facilitate the empowerment of service users, carers and other lay people to take some control of the research agenda in North and East Devon, without attempting to turn people into quasi-professionals. To do this, we need to work with academics and other professional researchers, as well as health and social care professionals, to reach a better understanding of what 'involvement ' really means. For Folk.us, involvement can be defined as: 'To be included on an equal basis. Participation in decisions which affect how much and what kind of support (or research people) receive (or take part in) ' (Lindow and Morris, 1995), and to shift the balance of power so that users and carers can initiate research in which professionals offer their skills and expertise in the service of users.

For research to have real value, it must address real issues and produce some level of solution or outcome (Baxter *et al.*, 2001). We also know that this is true in wider forms of user involvement. The 'Shaping Our Lives' project, an umbrella organisation of user-involvement organisations, produced a report after undertaking research on the outcomes of user involvement activities (Turner, 1998). The research found that service users should not only be involved in measuring outcomes but also in defining what those outcomes should be, and that the process of involvement should not, and cannot, be separated from outcomes. Though the 'Shaping Our Lives' study was concerned mainly with involvement in service provision and development, the findings can still be applied to involvement in research and the outcomes or results of research. We are working for user and lay involvement at all stages of the research process, including the implementation of research results. We believe this is the best way to produce results of integrity and value for all concerned.

By its very nature the research agenda tends to attract professionals rather than lay people, and initially, Folk.us attracted more professionals than service users. The service users, carers and lay people who have become involved tend to be well-informed about many aspects of research. Our challenge is to attract grassroots people who want to conduct or participate in research on their own terms, and who are willing to challenge the assumptions of professionals. Another difficulty for Folk.us is that we are not endorsing a particular approach to research, either in terms of paradigms or who should undertake the research. Our aim is for all research in health and social care in North and East Devon to address the issues of service users and/or carers and/or lay people, and that the agenda and process will be influenced and controlled meaningfully by service users and lay people. We assist service users and lay people in North and East Devon to undertake their own research, by offering a small amount of financial support, as well as ongoing advice and help with the research itself. We are committed to 'user-led ' and 'lay-led ' research as well as partnership, although the majority of our work is about bringing interested parties together and facilitating involvement in the research process.

User and carer involvement, as we know from past studies (Campbell and Oliver, 1996) can only work when we embrace the experiences of individuals. When people share experiences – for instance, of using health services – they often find common ground, and this can be the impetus for collective action. This process is no different when involving people in research. Folk.us has worked on the idea of bringing service users, professionals and lay people together to discuss common issues. However it is not always easy to find common issues when working with people with such different perspectives. We recognise that there are barriers to involvement, including inadequate physical access, lack of access to information in appropriate formats, and the use of jargon in meetings and documents (Lindow and Morris, 1995). The assumption that 'professionals know best ', and sometimes differences in fundamental values between professionals and service users/lay people, are also challenges.

Every organisation committed to involvement has to address these issues bearing in mind their particular circumstances. For example, we need to understand that holding Folk.us meetings within the University of Exeter may not create a sense of equality between lay people, service users and carers when faced with professionals, even though the ground floor where meetings take place has good physical access. The language of research is often inaccessible, and can be very difficult to translate. These are just some of the areas Folk.us is addressing to increase involvement in research.

Folk.us also faces the constant debate about whether lay people and service users are 'representative '. This is particularly hard for Folk.us, because we tend to be caught up in this argument in two different ways. Both have been applied when service users are research subjects or participants, or when they conduct their own research. The first argument is a general research issue and involves the 'research debate ' about qualitative research. There remains a widespread misunderstanding about representativeness in qualitative research. The point of qualitative research is that it explores in depth an individual experience within a particular context. The findings are not supposed to be 'representative', though they may be transferable to others in similar situations. Then we have the second argument around *who* is representative in terms of conducting research. Professional practitioners and researchers constantly request involvement from 'representative ' service users, carers and/or other lay people. The difficulty is that often the view held by professionals or researchers, or for that matter by other service users and lay people, about who is a representative user and/or lay person can be based more on 'stereotypical' images, rather than on real service users and/or lay people (Beresford and Campbell, 1994). Disabled people being seen as dependent or helpless, or carers as martyrs, are examples of images that have been challenged (Oliver, 1990; Shakespeare, 1997) but are still prolific in our society. We are constantly challenging the meaning of 'representative', as it is different for each project. After all, professional researchers are not required to be representatives of their social groups, so why should user-researchers?

Folk.us has the advantage of learning from the experience of social movements, where much of what we accept as good standards of user involvement was first established. There is little doubt that, had the women's movement, the black people 's movement and the disabled people 's movement not challenged power inequalities by, among other things, undertaking their own research activities, their issues would not have been addressed at any level (Solomos, 1993; Campbell and Oliver, 1996) and no policies would exist either to address or protect their rights, or to promote empowerment.

Particular Folk.us successes

Folk.us has been successful in facilitating projects in a number ways. The work we have been doing since our conception has included:

- Running an evolving programme of mutual learning events/workshops on various aspects of research and participation for mixed audiences;
- Researching and producing a leaflet on 'users as trainers' (Downs, 2001) which explores the views of service users and professionals when service users are involved in training professionals;
- Supporting a group of visually impaired people to undertake research about the services available to people when they are diagnosed with permanent sight loss. This is a joint project with Living Options Devon.
- Advising on the School Nurse Project run by North and East Devon Health Authority, which is evaluating the role of nurses in schools for children with challenging behaviour;
- Folk.us members are looking into the viability of a research proposal for a project to establish the service needs of people with physical impairments;
- Designing and establishing a joint agency policy on involving service users and lay people in research to be adopted by health and social care providers and commissioners of research;
- Supporting a Folk.us member to undertake research into writer 's cramp. This particular member suffered from writer's cramp himself, and the project received a grant from South West Region NHS Executive and was also supported by Exeter Council of Voluntary Services;
- Folk.us was commissioned by Consumers in NHS Research to undertake a 'scoping' study of lay involvement in research. This six-month project explored fields other than health, where service users, consumers and other stakeholders had been actively involved in research. It is intended that the findings of this project will be instrumental in informing NHS research policy in the future (Baxter *et al.*, 2001);
- Currently working with the North and East Devon NHS Research Ethics Committee to establish a process for gaining ethical approval and the consideration of user- and lay-person- led research initiatives;
- We have been invited to help with the recruitment of lay people and a researcher for a project to measure the quality of health by using a utility panel of lay people. This will be conducted by North and East Devon Directorate of Public Health;
- Designing a workshop on user involvement for health care managers and Primary Care Trust Executives, to take place in November this year;

- Folk.us successfully applied for funding from PPP Healthcare Medical Trust, to enable us to design and deliver a series of workshops called 'Your Services and Research – Making the Connection' to take place in North, East and Mid Devon. The aim is to raise awareness about research among service users, and 'grassroots ' health and social care staff. These will take place between October 2001 and January 2002; and
- Developing a policy for payment for service users and carers.

Other under-researched topics brought to our attention by lay people include: the physical abuse of people with learning disabilities; the experiences and treatment of adults with Asperger's syndrome; and the health scare stories of people admitted for acute care.

On a day-to-day basis we answer enquiries regarding involvement in research and maintain contact with both local and national organisations, such as the Mid Devon Research Group, Consumers in NHS Research Support Unit, and the Toronto Group, who focus on user involvement in social care research.

We disseminate our activities through our website http://latis.ex.ac.uk/folk.us and newsletter, Folk.us News. The website gives details of all our activities including our two- to three-monthly Folk.us Forum meetings and has links to other appropriate sites. Folk.us News is produced every two to three months, and is available in print or via the website.

What about the future?

User involvement in the provision and planning care services became a massive part of the social care agenda when the Services, Consultation and Representation Act (DHSS, 1986) was the first legislation to force consultation with service users and carers and voluntary agencies. This was again enforced in the NHS and Community Care Act 1990 (Oliver and Barnes, 1998). However, neither of these Acts included research. NHS Research Governance (Department of Health, 2000) is the first step to similar policy position, to involve and consult service users and lay people in research. The Research Governance states: 'Participants or their representatives should be involved wherever possible in the design, conduct, analysis and reporting of research' and that 'information must be presented in a format understandable to the public' (Department of Health, 2000).

Folk.us is already working towards both of these aims and we welcome the policy. This new framework, along with NHS research and development (R&D) expansion to incorporate social care and public health research will increase the demand for our expertise substantially, and this means we shall be under pressure to find new funding. At present we are trying to secure funding to increase the co-ordinator 's time from 2.5 days a week to 5 days, and for a part-time research adviser, just to meet current demand.

Future issues we will need to tackle include: further debate on quality in research (for example, what is good-quality research and whose standards should be used to judge it?); new work on innovative research methods for empowerment of people through research (for example, participatory appraisal, participatory action research), and broadening the criteria used by research ethics committees to incorporate users ' and carers ' concerns for mutual respect and empowerment. It is an exciting and challenging time for everyone with an involvement or interest in research and we should embrace it.

What have Folk.us members got out of the forum?

As Folk.us *is* its members, we approached people to make some comments about our work, and this is what three of our members said:

I have a physical difficulty which has caused me distress for many years. I had always found it hard to talk about. Folk.us was a place to go where I could 'open up' about my condition and explore ideas about doing my own research into it. What was crucial was the unconditional support and encouragement I received, from initial contact right the way through to doing an actual research project. It was this emotional support, as well as the practical help, that meant so very much to me. (service user)

Apart from a few 'users' who have opted for an academic career that encompasses research, few true service users have felt able to undertake work that might be regarded as research. Folk.us has set out to change this by demystifying research processes which will assist ordinary people to produce work that will sit alongside that produced by the more traditional methods. At the same time, Folk.us is working towards changing attitudes that will lead to the acceptance of research by users in those areas where it might be regarded with scepticism. Folk.us is altering the power balance in an inclusive and constructive way. This is a major stride forward and should help shape health and social care provision in years to come. (Leader of user group)

As my central theme had been to empower people, I was very enthusi-astic about the aims of Folk.us, but remembering my profound lack of knowledge of physical and other disabilities and lack of experience in social care, I initially felt very much a learner. I began to see what I knew that could be transferable to this new landscape. So not only has Folk.us taught me a lot but they have also enabled me to practice my skills. (Retired professional researcher, now lay member of Folk.us)

We are discovering that it is possible to 'do research together': it is time consuming, and it challenges taken-for-granted assumptions and values, but it is fun, rewarding, and it helps to break down the barriers of the academic ivory tower. We feel that this is a healthy approach to doing research.

Note

We would like to thank those members of Folk.us who gave us the quotes used in this chapter. Thanks are also extended to Lisa Thorne in the Folk.us office for her helpful comments on the draft for this contribution.

References

Baxter, L, Mitchell, A and Thorne, L (2001) *Small Voices, Big Noises: Lay involvement in research lessons learnt from other fields than health* Exeter, Washington Singer Press

Beresford, P and Campbell, J (1994) 'Disabled people, service users, user involvement and representation' *Disability and Society*, 9 (3)

Campbell, J and Oliver, M (1996) *Disability Politics* London, Routledge

Croft, S and Beresford, P (1993) *Getting Involved A practical guide for change* London, Open Services Project

Department of Health (2000) *Research Governance Framework* London, Crown Press

DHSS (Department of Health and Social Security) (1986) *Disabled Persons (Services, Consultation and Representation) Act 1986* London, Crown Press

Downs, S (2001) 'Understanding users as trainers' *Users Voices* Exeter, Folkus

Lindow, V and Morris, J (1995) *Service User Involvement* York, Joseph Rowntree Foundation

Oliver, M (1997) 'Emancipatory Research: Realistic goal or impossible dream?' in *Doing Disability Research* Barnes, C and Mercer, G (eds) Leeds, Disability Press

Oliver, M and Barnes, C (1998) *Disabled People and Social Policy from exclusion to inclusion* Harlow, Addison Wesley Longman

Orford, J (1992) *Community Psychology: Theory and Practice* Wiley

Shakespeare, T (1997) 'Cultural representation of disabled people for disavowal?' (first published 1994) *Disability Studies: Past, Present, Future* Leeds, Disability Press

Solomos, J (1993) *Race and Racism in Britain* London, Macmillan

Turner, M (1998) *Shaping Our Lives Project Report* London, National Institute for Social Work